The FARMHOUSE

The FARMHOUSE

New Inspiration *for the* Classic American Home

JEAN REHKAMP LARSON

Photographs by Ken Gutmaker

The Taunton Press

Text © 2006 by Jean Rehkamp Larson
Photographs © 2006 by Ken Gutmaker, except © Grey Crawford (pp. 2–3), © Stephanie Rau (back cover author photo)
Illustrations © 2006 by The Taunton Press, Inc.

The Farmhouse was originally published in hardcover in 2004 by The Taunton Press, Inc.

The Taunton Press
Inspiration for hands-on living®

The Taunton Press, Inc., 63 South Main Street, PO Box 5506, Newtown, CT 06470-5506
e-mail: tp@taunton.com

Editors: Roger Yepsen, Peter Chapman
Jacket/Cover design: Susan Fazekas
Interior design and layout: Susan Fazekas
Illustrator: Christine Erikson
Photographer: Ken Gutmaker

Library of Congress Cataloging-in-Publication Data
Larson, Jean Rehkamp.
  The farmhouse : new inspiration for the classic American home / Jean Rehkamp Larson.
      p. cm.
  ISBN-13: 978-1-56158-666-0 hardcover
  ISBN-10: 1-56158-666-8 hardcover
  ISBN-13: 978-1-56158-874-9 paperback with flaps
  ISBN-10: 1-56158-874-1 paperback with flaps
1. Farmhouses--Conservation and restoration--United States. 2. Farm buildings--Conservation and restoration--United States. 3.
Architecture--United States--21st century. I. Title.
  NA8208.5.L37 2004
  728'.6'0973--dc22
                            2004005981

Printed in Singapore
10 9 8 7 6 5 4 3
TWP   2009

The following manufacturers/names appearing in *The Farmhouse* are trademarks: Corian®, Maytag®

TO MY FAMILY

Acknowledgments

THE PROCESS OF CREATING SOMETHING involves many people, and I am thankful to all who worked to make this book happen. As an architect, I cannot help but compare this new experience of writing a book to the process that I know well—designing and building a house. In both cases, a group of people come together and envision what could be and then begin the exciting process of making it real. I have three groups of people to thank—the construction team, the support team, and the homeowners and architects.

The construction team is the people who worked hands-on to shape the words and images of this book. Roger Yepsen, the editor, respectfully encouraged me from start to finish, adding his thoughtful insight along the way. At The Taunton Press, I particularly wish to thank Maria Taylor for getting me started; Peter Chapman for his vision and experience crafting words and images; and Paula Schlosser and Susan Fazekas for a fresh visual layout. Ken Gutmaker, the photographer, captured just the right light and made friends with homeowners along the way. Susan Nackers Ludwig helped me scout and organize projects, laying the groundwork for the writing to follow.

A good support team is essential in any endeavor. I am ever thankful to my patient sounding board, Mark, who helped carve out space from a full life for this book, and also to my sons, Andrew and Peter, who each want their own copy. My extended family gave encouragement and additional slack in the chain when it was needed. Sarah Susanka and Dale Mulfinger, who are mentors from the world of architecture and Taunton authors themselves, provided valuable perspective.

I owe much to the homeowners and architects who graciously shared their houses and stories so that I was able to "get inside" and understand each farmhouse design featured here. Without their generosity, there would be no book. And finally, I thank Susan and Dave Marek for the opportunity to help them design their farmhouse. Their project, early in my career, led to this book as well as many other good things along the way.

Contents

Introduction

When The Taunton Press contacted me about writing a book on farmhouses, I sat down to consider just what makes the style so appealing to me. I recalled that as a young architect some years ago, I'd had my first opportunity to draw on this rural inspiration when Susan and Dave Marek walked in the door. They wanted to build on 11 acres of old farmland, and our ideas quickly took the form of a Midwestern farmhouse reconfigured for the way that people live today (see photos on this page and facing page).

As we worked together, I realized that farmhouses interest the urban dweller and small town girl in me, not just the architect. I attribute this to several dualities inherent in the style. A farmhouse is elegant yet simple. It is casual and welcoming but has the formality of symmetry and a confident stature. A farmhouse represents an idyllic agrarian life, yet it serves as the home base for a hardworking, notoriously gritty way of life. It serves as a link between the cultivated countryside and the city. These are qualities that I aspire to achieve in architecture and in life, and the farmhouse embodies a balance of each.

In practical terms, the simple, hearty form of the style is highly adaptable. A farmhouse can easily be expanded because the basic shapes make it easy to add porches, sheds, and wings. These houses can also be dressed up or dressed down, depending on what you expect from a home; the gable ends, soffits, and porch columns

can be left austere or filled with texture, trim, and detail.

This book provided the opportunity for me to survey the ways in which other architects are interpreting the style. I was curious—what does the next generation of farmhouses look like? Is the form in danger of evolving beyond recognition? As photographs and floor plans came in from around the country, I was impressed that these were not anachronistic attempts to capture a way of life that no longer exists. The houses represent the sophisticated development of this classic house type, with designs and materials as varied as the climates and cultures of our broad nation.

I hope this book will inspire you to take Sunday drives along rural roads in search of your own place in the country. Roll down the windows, listen to the crickets, and take in the long views as you envision your own unique version of the great American farmhouse.

After purchasing farm-
land used for grazing
cattle, the owners of this
farmhouse spent years
restoring the prairie wildflowers and grasses
before even considering
the design of the building.
As a result, the new
farmhouse looked imme-
diately settled in its site.

An American Icon

THE FARMHOUSES OF MY MEMORY stand tall on the Minnesota
prairie with their white clapboard walls and welcoming
porches. These are proud homes that stake out a piece of
landscape, braving the thunderstorms and snowdrifts of the Mid-
west. With the population shifts of past years, many of these
graceful structures now are neglected and in a state of decay. But I
continue to admire the clarity of their form, the idiosyncratic details, and the community they establish with their outbuildings.
Each farmstead seems to have gathered itself in a cluster for comfort and safety under the endless prairie sky.

I'm happy to say that the farmhouse, after years of decline, is
making a comeback. Even though fewer people now farm to make
a living, the style endures because we have come to see it as a classic symbol of home—an unforgettable feature of the American
landscape. Many of us continue to carry around the image of a bucolic white house glimpsed on a hill from a favorite country road.
And the familiar elements of the style—a gable roof, crisp lines,
and just enough detailing—are finding their way into new homes.

Across the country, people think of a farmhouse as a simple
box with double-hung windows, clad in clapboard, and
painted white. With their tall, proud proportions, these
houses make a strong domestic statement in the rural
landscape.

Double-hung windows are typical of a traditional farmhouse, but in this room the units are oversized and ganged together within a boldly vaulted space. The trusses draw on tradition as well—they were inspired by old-world barns.

The traditional gable forms are given a modern edge with corrugated metal siding, a checkerboard roof, and dark-colored windows without muntins.

Synonymous with Shelter

The farmhouse style goes beyond nostalgia. A farmhouse offers the promise of reconnecting with natural rhythms—with the four seasons and the cycles of life. Whether it is in a soybean field or a subdivision, a farmhouse can be an antidote to a commercialized, information-glutted world. For many homeowners, it represents a chance to get back to the basics—finding a reasonable pace in a time when mainstream culture seems to be accelerating.

Throughout this book you'll find successful ways of both rethinking older houses and also starting from scratch. As you can see, the results of the two approaches are often indistinguishable. The homes have in common a solidity and a measure of grace that identifies them as heirs to the farmhouse tradition. A renovated Michigan farmhouse received a bold checkerboard roof and walls wrapped with corrugated metal siding (see the bottom photo at left and pp. 166–175). And a new house in Massachusetts combines details from historic Shaker buildings with a vaulted barnlike great room (see top photo at left and pp. 204–213).

A Home-Grown Style

In early photos, farming families often posed in front of their houses because shelter was so crucial to their survival. Those four walls held them safe within a broad, unknown continent. Although there no longer are unexplored frontiers, many of us still think of the farm as a refuge—a safe environment that is grounded in purity, honesty, and simple virtues. Perhaps for this reason, our children are introduced to the farmyard in storybooks, movies, and cartoons.

As adults, we are drawn to the democratic spirit of a style that isn't associated with an elite class or a particular region. No matter their size or how proper and pressed they may appear, farmhouses are unlikely to be pretentious or showy.

The farmhouse is uniquely American, despite the fact that the style has been influenced over the centuries by European traditions. English Colonial homes contributed symmetry, the gable roof, and the double-hung window. The Greek Revival style gave us classical details and lots of white paint. Stone farmhouses are found in the German-settled areas of eastern Pennsylvania. In the Deep South, the French influence can be seen in farmhouses with glass-paned doors, paired windows, and hipped roofs with a steep pitch.

On a farmhouse, porches are important as a transition space between home life and farmyard. This porch serves as another room, providing fresh air and open views while maintaining a sense of refuge. It also stands as a clear symbol of welcome.

Practical, humble materials like concrete floors and exposed concrete block are a good fit for a rural house. In this Midwestern farmhouse, the horizontal lines of the landscape are echoed by the open shelves and long built-in between kitchen and living room.

There are regional differences, too, because designs were often modified on the spot to suit the family's particular needs and the nature of the site. In New England, outbuildings were often grafted right onto the farmhouse so that the family wouldn't have to step out into the brutal winter weather when tending animals. Farmhouses of the West responded to the open landscape and strong light with generous porches

and deep overhangs. And in the South, you are apt to see farmhouses elevated on piers to let cooling breezes blow through.

Each house takes on the imprint of the people who lived there, resulting in a truly *vernacular* style—one that adapts to local needs and preferences. That's why you are unlikely to find two identical farmhouses. Like snowflakes, they may seem the same at first glance but then reveal

Because the garage on this Western farm is detached, it was possible to make the footprint of the house smaller. In both size and roof shape, the two buildings are similar to the barn and relate well to it, reinforcing the sense of a rural enclave.

countless variations when given a closer look. This quirky individuality is one of the most endearing characteristics of farmhouses.

Hallmarks of the Farmhouse Style

It's interesting to look at the key features of farmhouses around the country. These characteristics can help us design new homes that respectfully relate to the surrounding environment, that are tastefully simple in shape in color, and that have the mix of forms and textures that suggest a home has gracefully evolved over the years.

ONE WITH THE LAND

Farmhouses are placed with care upon the landscape, unlike the rigid way in which suburban houses are plunked around their cul-de-sacs. The traditional wisdom was to choose a site that protected the home from midday sun and harsh weather. Each part of the country has arrived at its own version of this strategy.

In the handmade spirit of quirky rural structures, the simple symmetrical form of this Midwestern farmhouse has an embellishment at the peak of the gable end.

As direct and purposeful as a plowed furrow, two-wheel tracks guide the eye through the cornfield to the front door of an old farmhouse.

With a tall central gable and low-pitched roofs to either side, this house is something of a cross between a traditional gabled farmhouse and a simple utility shed. Corrugated galvanized siding also links the house to the hardworking outbuildings of the farm.

On the Midwestern prairie, farmers plant groves of trees to block the winter winds that roar down out of Canada. In the arid Southwest, farm buildings gather around a well or stream as if to take a long drink, while trees provide shade at the hottest time of day. When the climate and terrain are taken into consideration, even a new farmhouse can look as though it belongs in its setting rather than being superimposed there.

Pasture and out-buildings almost seem to be part of the furnishings of this glass-walled addition. In dramatic contrast to the adjacent farmhouse, the modern living room pavilion is set flush with the grass, minimizing the boundary between inside and out.

The vestige of a stone chimney on the bedroom wall of this renovated Texas farmhouse is a reminder that an old stove was needed before central heat. It is likely that the smaller of the two windows provided ventilation and light for a former attic.

The new addition to this farmhouse fits well in the composition of existing outbuildings. The gable shape, with its two traditional windows aligned below the ridge, keeps one foot in the past. Nevertheless, the voids below the overhang and a tall window with no muntins at the corner hint that there is more to the story.

HONEST MATERIALS

Because farmers were necessarily frugal, they didn't overlook building materials close at hand. Their houses quite literally sprang up from the soil. The by-products of clearing the fields included fieldstone, used for foundations and walls, as well as trees, which were locally hewn and milled into beams, clapboard, shingles, and flooring.

Today, we have a renewed appreciation for regional building materials. There is an environmental advantage to using them and an aesthetic benefit, too. Traditional materials help intimately tie a new home to its unique place in the world. That might mean cedar shakes in New England, slate roofs in Vermont, brick in Indiana, clapboard in Missouri, and adobe in New Mexico. There's no need to follow tradition slavishly as if it were a building code, of course, but it's hard to go far wrong with components that have been with us for hundreds of years.

SIMPLE FORMS

The phrase "form follows function" wasn't coined by an American farmer—but it might have been. It is an idea that clearly had a hand in shaping our rural architecture. Both the proportions and the scale of the farmhouse were arrived at long ago for practical reasons. The right-angled walls and 45-degree roof pitches are easily framed, without complex calculation or sophisticated tools. And the pieces from which these homes were built— studs, rafters, stones—are small enough for one or two people to haul around and set into place. This direct, logical approach continues to produce beautifully proportioned houses today. As with design in general, limitations can have an aesthetic benefit, guarding against excess and frills.

THE RURAL PALETTE

As anyone would know from taking a drive through the countryside, rural paint schemes were kept as simple as the forms they adorn— white for the house and red for the barn, with accents for doors and shutters.

This paired-down approach saved time, and the pigments in white and red paint were cheap. There may be a historical reason behind the white farmhouse, as well. Even though farmers were relatively isolated from architectural fads, their

This house has the familiar look of a barn and a farmhouse rolled into one, for a novel form that is refreshingly different. The upper and lower windows are aligned to help maintain a pure, uncluttered simplicity.

Simple white- and red-painted forms are emblematic of the farm. By keeping trim and siding the same color, the emphasis remains on the pleasing design of the window composition and the overall proportions.

A farmhouse seems most at home when accompanied by outbuildings of varying shapes and sizes. These structures sprang up over time as needed, but a new farmstead can be laid out to have that same comfortably settled appearance.

This new Greek revival farmhouse looks as though the central core came first and then was followed by a succession of later wings and porches. Shifts of roofline and materials help to suggest that a home has evolved over time.

While decks often look as though they were tacked on, this one works as an exterior living room. It's anchored by a masonry fireplace, wrapped with a railing, and lit by attractive fixtures.

white homes may be in part the legacy of the all-white Greek Revival style, which spread from the cities to the countryside back in the mid 1800s.

There is more to these color choices than economy and fashion. The monochromatic paint scheme of a farmhouse draws attention to its elegantly straightforward form. Upon closer inspection you can appreciate the intriguing textures and patinas of the siding, trim, and detailing. Also, white is often seen as the color of hope and optimism. It has a way of making an unadorned house look poised and self-confident. And white walls offer a refreshingly clean, civilized break from the mud and manure of rural life.

When there is no barn on the site, some farmhouse owners choose the signature deep red of the barn for their homes. And barn-red paint, hardwearing and made from a humble ore, has its own aura of unselfconscious practicality.

GROWN OVER TIME

Unlike most manufactured things, houses are dynamic, changing over the years in response to their owners' needs and to the effects of the elements. The former front entry might have been relegated to a side door when the farm lane was relocated. Unwanted windows may disappear beneath new siding. Stairways and interior walls tend to be shifted over time, and bathrooms materialize in a floor plan that predates plumbing.

Older farmhouses have imbedded histories that draw us in with their stories of the past, and new owners are likely to discover all sorts of curious wrinkles. While renovating the vintage Massachusetts farmhouse on pp. 30–39, the owners found a traditional "concealment shoe" tucked within the masonry of the fireplace to ensure good fortune for the occupants; this chance

discovery is the tactile sort of connection that we can have with the people who long ago walked the very same floorboards as we do. Stories like these animate four walls, so that a home becomes a rich place in which to live.

Similarly, a new farmhouse can *imply* a history by suggesting that it has grown wings, porches, and dormers over the years. For example, the California farmhouse shown in the middle photo on the facing page (and on pp. 60–69) has a dominant Greek Revival center, flanked by modest wings that appear to have been added at a later date. Wings have practical advantages, too. Because they tend to be narrow, with windows on at least two sides, they often have plenty of light and good air circulation.

The Mississippi farmhouse on pp. 186–193 seems to have a conventional wraparound porch within which a screened area and a galley kitchen have been added, but in fact these features were part of the original design. Another effective device is simply to change the height of the roof ridge, or the roof's pitch. Smaller details also can give the impression that a home has morphed over time. Architects will switch to another material or finish from one part of the house to the other or use hardware that appears to be from another era.

A new farmhouse designed in this way can have enough space to met today's many needs—master bath, walk-in closet, family room—and still remain humble and unpretentious. By breaking up the form in various ways, architects avoid presenting an imposing facade to the world. You *can* have it both ways—a spacious home in the best farmhouse tradition.

A Farmhouse Loves Company

Picture a farmhouse, and you probably imagine a barn as well. And maybe a silo, windmill, corncrib, and a chicken coop or two. These outbuildings are architectural forms in their own right. Each has a distinctive form that is born of its purpose. Many barns have a double-pitched gambrel roof that looks as though it were pushed upward by a big harvest of hay, and in fact this configuration

Outbuildings can be converted for new uses as guest quarters, a workshop, or a home office, allowing the farmyard to remain intact and functional. The straightforward structures make a good backdrop for the color and texture of flower and vegetable gardens.

The arrangement of the buildings on a new farmstead can draw inspiration from the rural traditions of the region. The architect of this house admired groupings of historic tobacco barns lined up neatly in a row, an image that became a starting point for the home's design.

A new farmhouse doesn't have to be a replication of a historic style. Here, casement windows, horizontal trim, and open vaulted rooms create a clean, airy interior. The industrial corrugated siding inside makes a connection with the property's hardworking barn.

encloses more space than a standard gable roof. The slatted sides of a corncrib help dry and preserve ears of field corn for use throughout the year. Windmills and water towers also make their mark on the land. Each structure symbolizes a way of life that is fast vanishing from much of the country.

A farmhouse that serves as a weekend retreat or retirement home may not need a full complement of barns and silos, of course. Still, the property can be given a settled look with such structures as a detached garage, storage shed, guest quarters, or studio workshop. These outbuildings are attractive getaway spaces where the family can be playful and untidy—perfect for an adult's projects or a child's playhouse. A new building can be given a traditional shape, or you might prefer to have it honestly express its modern role.

Whatever their style or purpose, the nestled buildings of a farmstead create a sense of community, especially if they are arranged in a coordinated way. On a working farm, the barn would be placed downwind from the home, chicken coops would face the sun, and an outbuilding might shelter the garden from sharp winds. In laying out the grounds of a new home, the farmhouse and its outbuildings can be situated artfully, framing some views and concealing others so that they are dramatically revealed only as visitors approach. In this way, buildings are treated as elements of the landscape, with a pleasing logic of their own.

This new entryway is a mix of interior and exterior details. The white horizontal siding and the stone are typical of a farmhouse exterior, while across the hall a wall of raised-panel cabinetry is a classic interior Colonial detail.

The Future of the Farmhouse

The farmhouse style isn't a formula, with a fixed inventory of features, but a setting for a way of life, and this is the heart of its lasting appeal. Farmhouses continue to inspire homeowners and architects alike as a familiar, approachable alternative that can be adapted to modern-day preferences—informal floor plans, generous windows, inviting bedrooms, and kitchens designed for relaxed entertaining. With a scale and appearance that were shaped by necessity, these homes satisfy a longing for a wholesome, satisfying life grounded in a sense of the land and its traditions.

The projects in this book show just how far the notion of the farmhouse can be stretched and interpreted without losing touch with its quiet, understated spirit. There are classical, hearty farmhouses, playfully stark modern farmhouses, and many variations in between. You may be inspired to find your own improvisation on this durable theme, incorporating your unique vision while embracing America's rural heritage.

In the evening, the warm glow from a farmhouse on an open landscape is a beacon of domestic comfort. The shelter of the deep wraparound porch feels especially welcome at twilight.

While the barn is all business and economy, the house seems to grow up out of the windswept plains with its low-pitched, intersecting shed roofs leaning against a tall gable.

A PORTFOLIO *of* FARMHOUSES

The jumbled forms of the porch and the kitchen bump-out lend a less formal character to the rear of the house.

An Unsentimental Farmhouse

T HE SITE OFTEN HELPS SHAPE the design of the home that will be built on it. That was the case with Cathy's new farmhouse in the Hudson Highlands of New York State. The open field on the property suggested a straightforward house "without fanfare," she says. From the start, Cathy decreed that there would be no front porch and no shutters.

Even a driveway didn't fit in. Cathy guessed that an attached garage or adjacent parking area would work against the stillness she hoped to enjoy as she approached the house. So cars are now parked here and there in a grassy field, looking as placid as grazing cows. The white house sits prominently above, atop a rise backed by a green curtain of woods. A stone wall borders the small yard around the house, providing definition between lawn and field.

This white clapboard farmhouse stands out like an icon against a dark backdrop of trees. The familiar elements of the style have been rejuvenated by arranging the home's elements at unconventional angles.

21

Straight Up, with a Twist

The house is composed of a tall central structure, a wing, and a back porch—with an interesting alignment. The forms may all be conventional, but they intersect at odd angles. Architect David Bers jumbled them in a deconstructed, playful way that ensured the house wouldn't become a stagnant replica of a beloved style.

Still, there are enough familiar elements to place the home in the farmhouse tradition: double-hung windows, a gable roof, a prominent front door, and wood siding. The main part of the house has corner boards that hint at the *pilasters* typical of the Greek Revival style—columns that project somewhat from the wall, topped with trim called a *capital*.

These elements take on an edge, again by subtly defying expectations. Double-hung windows are placed with a modern rigor. They are symmetrically stacked, three over three, creating a facade with an abstractly geometric pattern. Their undivided panes avoid any hint of nostalgia while providing an unobstructed view of the property. The front door pushes out from its corner at an unexpected angle. And around in back, a cantilevered bump-out increases the usable floor space of the kitchen. Along with the skewed porch, these features deviate just enough from standard operating procedure to keep the house on its toes.

Where you might expect to see a front porch, a set of broad wood steps marches to the door. They are patterned after the houses in Nantucket, where Cathy spends her summers. Their generous size makes them an inviting place to sit and soak up the sun while waiting for guests. The front door is flanked by sidelights, wide boxy pilasters, and a horizontal *entablature* above, all classic Greek Revival elements rendered in a stylized way.

Folklore has it that yellow jackets won't build nests on a blue ceiling because it looks like the sky to them. The ornate chandelier is a playful counterpoint to the informality of the exposed rafters and tongue-and-groove ceiling.

The seams of the stainless-steel roof highlight the well-composed misalignment of the home's wing and porch, making them appear to be later additions.

A tall foundation helps the house hold its own with the towering trees just beyond.

Full-height sidelights are a traditional way of adding daylight to an otherwise darkened entryway, even when the front door is closed. The well-polished concrete floors make the most of the daylight, reflecting it into the hall.

Located three steps up from the main floor, the study is removed just enough from day-to-day activities to make working from home an attractive option. The room's lower ceiling and muted green paint give it the feeling of a retreat tucked away within the house.

Paring Down to Lighten Up

Inside, Cathy called for a layout that would encourage a simple way of living and working. Good proportions and quality materials mean that no bells and whistles were needed. The *program,* or list of spaces to be included, was pared down to the essentials—no formal dining room and just two bedrooms sharing a bath upstairs. David's design is modest in size, but high ceilings and tall windows help make it seem larger than 2,000 sq. ft. Also, the use of "view corridors" that lead the eye into adjacent rooms and out to the landscape beyond adds to the sense of spaciousness.

Because the rooms are interrelated, there is no sense of living in a series of boxes.

The entry hall extends right through the house, leading to a floor-to-ceiling sheet of glass that allows the view to keep going into the woods beyond. The curious kinks of the design become evident as you proceed down the irregularly shaped hall, although the rooms to each side are the traditional rectilinear spaces. Their materials and detailing are traditional, too, but in a simplified, unfussy way. Moldings have a straightforward look, the living room bookcases aren't embellished with trim, and the clarity of the

As with the trim throughout the house, the lines of the bookshelves are clean and simple. The strong order in the room is a contrast to the adjacent free-flowing entry hall.

With its 9-ft. ceilings and tall windows, the second level of the home feels more spacious than its square footage would suggest. The antique pierced-tin pie safe finds a new job storing linen in the gallery-like upper hall.

Wide-open double doors dissolve the boundary between kitchen and porch, although the unusual angle at which the porch meets the house is obvious to the eye. In contrast, a thickened wall emphasizes the threshold into the living room.

A Modern Angle on Tradition

WHEN DESIGNING A HOUSE, architects explore three-dimensional space with two-dimensional drawings—plans, sections, and elevations. These drawings dissect the house in different ways, just as cutting an apple from top to bottom and side to side will give two very different images. A look at the jumbled blocks of this house's plan brings to mind unconventional buildings by Modern architects such as Frank Gehry, while the section of the gable is the familiar archetype of an American house. As the drawings suggest, the final three-dimensional form is a combination—a classic house with a modern sensibility.

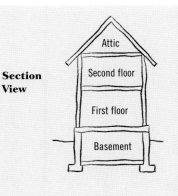

Section View

Attic

Second floor

First floor

Basement

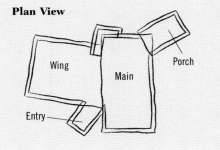

Plan View

Wing

Main

Porch

Entry

An inviting stair spills down from a landing into the hall. The wood treads and handrail provide a warm contrast to the concrete floor and white walls.

design is preserved by using humble pull-down roller shades instead of flouncy curtains.

The paint colors maintain the theme of tradition with a spin. That can be difficult to pull off just by eyeballing paint chips, and Cathy brought in a paint-and-plaster expert to consult with her in "editing" the color palette, as she puts it.

Although David avoided sentimental gestures by designing this home with such broad strokes, Cathy did have pieces of older furniture from her mother that needed a sympathetic setting. The symmetry and order of the well-proportioned rooms ensure that the architecture does not overwhelm these treasured pieces.

The kitchen draws more attention to itself, with the cantilevered bay to accommodate the sink and counters. A pair of casement windows flank a square center pane—a departure from the windows used elsewhere. The soffit above is

The blue soffit calls attention to the skewed roof of the kitchen's bay. This bumped-out wall made it possible to place a good-size table in the center of the room. The windows above the sink wrap around the corner of the bay so that light enters from two sides.

Farmhouse L's and T's

Drive across rural America, and you may notice that many farmhouses have a one-and-a-half or two-story central structure with a perpendicular wing. Viewed from above, the two parts create the shape of either an L or a T. The wing typically was added as a farm family grew. This expansion was symbolic, too, representing the family's success in working the surrounding land.

Adding a wing offers the opportunity to reorganize the existing rooms and improve the overall layout. For example, a new kitchen wing might allow converting the old kitchen into a dining room or living room, making daily life a bit more gracious. Another advantage of a wing is that its rooms extend out from the core structure and typically have at least two exterior walls for natural light and air. Also, the intersection of a home and its wing creates a good spot to nestle a porch. New houses can benefit from this tradition—joining two gable forms to create a design that is economical, efficient, and more than the sum of its parts.

painted a robin's egg blue, as a tie to the striking exposed-joist ceiling of the adjacent porch. Cathy was intent on using slate—real slate, not a modern interpretation—for the countertops and backsplash, and the near-black stone adds some depth to the otherwise light-hearted room.

David assured Cathy that the screen porch would not strike her as suburban, and with its orderly white columns, it does look something like a small Greek temple in the woods. Because the porch is perched at an angle to the house, it appears to be a later addition, which in turn suggests that the house dates back much further than 1998.

Cathy was aware that her initial dream easily could have been obscured by adding the usual resale features, such as lots of bedrooms and bathrooms, a separate dining room, and a kitchen island. She credits the success of this project to maintaining a clear image and not relenting in the face of convention.

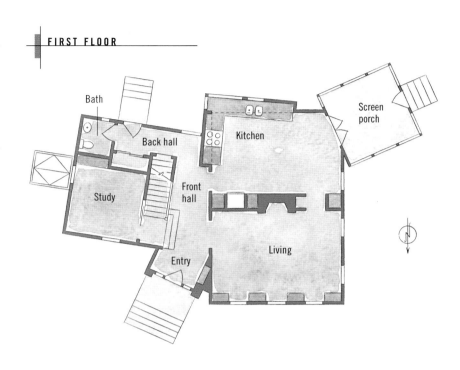

FIRST FLOOR

A Bicentennial Renovation

The scattering of outbuildings is tied together by the shared use of weathered wood siding and shingles. The grazing fields, shingled buildings, and stone walls create a composition of time-eased edges rather than hard lines.

MARTHA'S VINEYARD, off the Massachusetts coast, is better known for summer houses than for its few remaining working farms. But the island's agricultural history lives on at Clarissa and Mitchell's farm. They sell organic poultry, eggs, and lamb; and the wool from the 150 sheep that graze their pastures is made into sweaters, hats, and blankets for sale at the farm's small store.

The 100-acre property has been in Clarissa's family since before the Revolution, making it one of the oldest and largest farms on the island. Clarissa remembers when her grandmother lived in the house, with a hand pump and a cast-iron stove in the kitchen and a Maytag® ringer washer in the yard. After spending many summers there as a teenager, Clarissa moved in full time in her twenties. By then, the barns were all in disrepair. So was the Colonial house, built by her ancestors in 1773 and never extensively remodeled (plumbing wasn't added until the 1970s).

Wraparound casement windows connect the kitchen to the action in the yard. The skylights were a departure from an otherwise careful historic renovation; the owners wanted a few sun-filled spaces to balance the contained feeling of the original rooms.

Clarissa and Mitchell have restored miles of stone walls, and they continue to add more as a way of defining fields and containing livestock. There is no shortage of granite in the grazing fields.

A Kitchen Sink Vision

It took Clarissa and Mitchell a good while to figure out how to improve the historic property. One day Clarissa happened to be standing in the yard, looking past the barns to the sheep pastures, and she found herself thinking that this was the view she wanted from the kitchen sink. Having windows at that spot would bring sunlight into the kitchen and also allow her to see customers approaching the wool shop on the property. The idea was simple enough, but it proved to be the seed for the entire project.

SITE PLAN

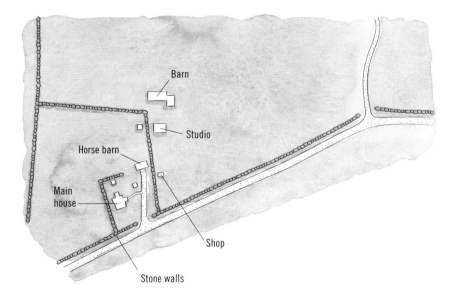

Local builder Mark Hurwitz had erected two barns for the family, and he was hired to collaborate in the ambitious expansion and renovation. The job began dramatically, by lifting up the old house and then building a new foundation for both it and the additions to come. Next, the carpenters took on the painstaking work of tying a new timber frame to the original structure. This crew was made up of former boatbuilders, and they had an intuitive sense of what looks good and works well. They cut the timbers on site, then assembled them with pegged mortise-and-tenon joints like those in the old house.

The sign on the gate quietly shoos away unannounced visitors who might mistake the farm for a living museum. The small stone-and-shingle building was used by English settlers to dry out peat for use as fuel.

The home looks well settled in, even though it was greatly expanded not long ago. The stone wall and outbuildings help establish that the farmhouse has been there a very long time.

Melding Colonial and Contemporary

The entire structure was reshingled, blending the new work with the old. Although the front door is rarely used, it was taken apart, refurbished, and reassembled. The central chimney needed to be rebuilt as well. As its bricks crumbled over the years (they likely had been used as ballast in sailing ships), new bricks were simply placed over them, so that the fireplace openings became increasingly smaller. In the process of dismantling some 6,000 bricks, the crew discovered an old pegged "concealment shoe" hidden in the masonry—it was an English tradition to put a shoe in the chimney for good luck. This shoe now has a revered spot on the mantel, and one of Mitchell's boots took its place to guarantee continued good fortune. The old bricks were

Upstairs, the line between old and new is marked in the hall by the change from a flat to a vaulted ceiling. A long wall of cabinets provides storage for linens, and the wood's white finish reflects light to take full advantage of the skylight and window.

New England Colonial

There isn't a single, consistent style of Colonial house. Each region's colonists borrowed forms and building techniques from their native country. In the English colonies, the Renaissance-inspired Georgian style was brought over from the old country.

Clarissa and Mitchell's farmhouse is an example—a simple rectangular box, two stories high and one or two rooms deep, with some detail at the front door and cornice. Because these houses were constructed before mass-produced lumber was available, they have a handmade feel about them. This home originally was a modest "half Colonial," so called because only two timber-frame bays were built, with the intention of adding a

third in the future. When the couple launched into a major renovation more than 200 years later, the house finally took on its intended form. The front facade is now symmetrical, with a centered front door and double-hung windows neatly stacked.

As often was the practice in older homes, interior walls and doors were of frame-and-panel construction. The stripped wood has a warm patina that complements the freshly painted wainscoting.

In keeping with traditional construction, the doors and drawers of the kitchen cabinets are set within the frame and have exposed hinges and wooden pulls. The green hue matches a color of milk paint that Clarissa discovered when stripping old doors for the house.

used on the visible portions of the rebuilt fireplace as well as for a new chimney stack in the kitchen.

The new section at the front of the house includes a double-purpose study and guest room on the first floor and a master bedroom suite upstairs. An addition to the rear takes the form of an open space for the dining room and kitchen; its timber-frame construction defines the two rooms and also links them visually with the original house. While Clarissa and Mitchell wanted to maintain their home's intimate, small-scale

While the kitchen is a new space, the mix of materials gives it the look of having evolved over time. The butcher block, open shelves, and exposed framing help tie the room to the rest of the house.

charm, they welcomed the chance to make these new areas bright and airy, including skylights and wraparound windows to take in views of the Atlantic. By designing this addition to be open with views back into the old house, they helped ensure that the entire home feels rooted in the past.

The Kitchen as Workplace

In the kitchen, modern appliances are paired with a traditional style of painted cabinet doors and drawer fronts, suggesting that only the appliances are of recent vintage. The painted base cabinets seem more like furniture than conventional built-in cabinetry. An intentional mix of

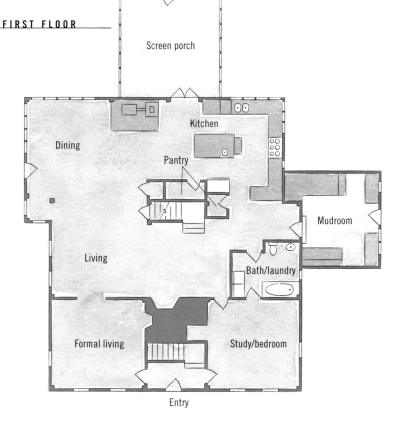

FIRST FLOOR

Screen porch

Dining

Kitchen

Pantry

Living

Mudroom

Bath/laundry

Formal living

Study/bedroom

Entry

The light-filled dining room straddles past and present. The addition has large, plentiful windows in the manner of a contemporary house, while the timber frame and wide-plank flooring align it with the era of the original home. The double-hungs were custom made with true divided lights to match those used in the older rooms.

The proud house stoops down to receive guests informally at this side door. As on the original house, the simple window trim is painted a subtle gray that blends in with the weathered shingles. A large stone slab from the property serves as the stoop at the end of the brick walk.

Pine from the site was hand hewn for the mudroom's timber frame. The cantilevered wood bench, left with a natural curve from the sawn log, feels like an extension of the frame.

different countertops—Corian®, wood, and granite—gives the room a worn and eclectic feel, as does the freestanding butcher block.

Two large walk-in pantries easily make up for the upper cabinets sacrificed to allow plenty of windows (and the windows did manage to capture just the view that Clarissa had envisioned). Open shelves hold everyday dishes, and the kitchen is illuminated by no-nonsense exterior lamps, with rugged green enamel shades, and by a strategically placed skylight. The quarry-tile floor is all business as well.

Working the land means bringing a bit of the soil inside with each trip through the door. The rear addition was planned so that the first stops are a mudroom, with its wooden grates to intercept dirt, and a bathroom with a shower and laundry area.

Throughout the process, Clarissa and Mitchell were clear about having the renovation honor the original Colonial, and Mark and the carpenters took cues from the original house as they worked with the structure. Along the way, the crew took the time to build custom window sashes and frames, to match the wood and nailing pattern of the original wide-plank floors, to peg the timber framing, and to use colors inspired by the coat of paint uncovered while stripping woodwork. While the house more than doubled in size, the change doesn't feel like a radical transformation so much as a completion of the original structure.

Living in a traditional style of home involves everyday tactile experiences. The feel of this door latch contributes to the character of the home in a small but very real way.

The Simple Life?

"DEPENDENCIES" WERE THE OUT-BUILDINGS that allowed early farms to be largely self-sufficient. Clarissa and Mitchell's farm continues in this tradition, and a tally of their many outbuildings might quickly cure you of any overly romantic notions about the simple joys of rural living. The assortment includes a chicken house, horse barn, maintenance and lambing building, knitting and weaving studio, woodworking shop, and wool shop. Each building is a physical marker of a task that must be carried out as part of the family's daily life and yearly cycles.

Little Red Barn House

M OST CLIENTS APPROACH AN ARCHITECT with clippings from home magazines. Thad and Sheila showed up at Geoff Warner's office with a children's book that had photos of simple red barns. The couple said they wanted a house that looked like a modern version of a barn.

For an architect, the term *modern* often connotes a flat roof, but Thad and Sheila felt strongly that a sloped gable roof was a good match for their rural site. Geoff took this requirement seriously. In the shop attached to his office, he cut a small block of wood to represent a stripped-down gable-roofed house, shorn of any traditional accouterments. Thad and Sheila liked what they saw, and Geoff was free to begin designing the details that would bring the initial concept into three-dimensional reality.

Playing with Expectations

Keeping the image of the wood model in mind, Geoff designed the typical features of the house in a not-so-typical way. The result seems straightforward at first glance, but there are unexpected, whimsical twists that bring you back for a second look.

From a distance, the red house looks like an object that was set down on the landscape. It's as if you could pick it up and feel its weight in the palm of your hand.

What appears from a distance to be barn-red siding is in fact plastic-laminated sheets, attached with stainless-steel screws—a high-tech, low-maintenance alternative to wood.

As a visitor approaches from the dirt road, the house shows a pair of eye-like upper windows on either side of a stucco-clad chimney that corresponds to a nose. (In fact, this feature serves a function other than carrying away smoke, as visitors discover when they step inside.) A typical farmhouse sits up on a foundation, but the siding of this house extends all the way to the ground; the structure looks as though it is floating in its surrounding moatlike border of dark rocks.

Because an overhanging roof can look like a cap placed on top of the walls, Geoff chose to have no overhang whatsoever, preserving the home's block-like unity. Nor are there any gutters to detract from the clean lines. Instead, rainwater passes *behind* the red panels that sheathe the house and drains down to the rock border below.

The rocks not only serve to carry off the water but also provide an alternative to the customary fringe of foundation plantings at the base of a house. Although the siding looks like stained 4-ft. by 8-ft. sheets of red plywood, it is a resin-impregnated product that requires no attention. Sheila and Thad envisioned a modern, low-maintenance house, and traditional white clapboard siding—with its need to be repainted periodically—simply was not in the running.

True to Form

The house is not without its own sort of adornment. Up close, the red walls appear to be zipped up in the middle and snapped together at the corners. The trim, tailored look comes from the rows of stainless-steel screws used to fasten the siding. They are expressed in some places and painted red to fade away in other locations.

The entry has the essential pieces—a durable tile floor, a bench, hooks, and a storage cabinet, all contained in one corner of the large open main floor space. The stair walls, with a natural stucco finish, are an extension of the exterior chimney form.

Without offering the amenities and frills of a traditional entryway, the wood bridge receives visitors like an oversized welcome mat. It looks as if one portion of the deck was elevated and folded to create the simple bench.

The owners wanted a comfortably modern house, not a cold white box. The simple base, cove, and window trim, along with the warm neutral tone of the walls, give this house an aesthetic that is at once clean and home-like.

The red metal windows on the second level are set flush with the siding, and they align with the wide red bands, emphasizing the uncomplicated shape of the house. With its stylized simplicity, this might be a fairy-tale house that would shelter Little Red Riding Hood. A wide wooden plank spans the moat of rocks like a drawbridge, marking the understated entrance with little fanfare. (The plank looks as though it could be pulled up if the Wolf happened by.)

The main level is devoted to one large space, with light coming in from openings on all four sides. The room's defining element is what appeared from the outside to be the oversized chimney. Instead, this is a stair tower, rising to the third level. There is a fire, but it is contained in a conventional freestanding stove on the other side of the room. Although the large space is free of interior walls, the living and dining areas are

The architect used resources wisely to get a good return on the money spent. The custom walnut cabinet and Corian countertop are paired with stock cabinets from a home furnishings chain.

The stairwell skylight is positioned to highlight the texture and uneven color of the natural stucco finish. The boards on the custom sliding barn-like doors are vertical on the bedroom side and horizontal on the hall side, giving the two rooms a subtly different character.

FIRST FLOOR

Kitchen

Dining

Patio

Wood-stove

Utility

Living room

Entry

The custom sink is a modern version of the large porcelain basins once found in older homes. The painted-out door trim, shadow-box storage niche, and stainless-steel cover plates build on the home's clean, modern lines.

subtly defined by a dropped section of ceiling, or *soffit,* running between the two.

The small kitchen occupies a corner of its own, and it avoids seeming sequestered by being kept visually open to the rest of the main level. A counter is all that sets off the sparely equipped food-preparation area. There is no need to hide away the kitchen because it is as uncluttered as the rest of the house.

On the second floor, the two bedrooms maintain the home's open feeling when their large barnlike doors are slid back. The bathroom, clad with maple panels, has the look of a box inserted between the bedrooms. The bath doesn't have an exterior window because of the flue chase from the stove below, but light comes in through long strips of glass set high on walls shared with the bedrooms. These interior windows add a sense

Master bedroom — Washer and dryer

Bunk room

With walls clad in maple, the bathroom looks like a box that was inserted into the bedroom. The recessed glass is devoid of traditional trim, so that it appears to be a slit cut through the side of the box.

A Matter of Scale

IN ARCHITECTURE, THE HUMAN BODY is the unit of measurement. That's because buildings are made to hold people. The term *scale* is used to describe how people relate to a building. And this red barn house ingeniously plays with these expectations, creating unexpected discoveries as you step inside. Because it is so simple, with only four openings per side, the house appears to be smaller than it is from a distance. This in turn allows the wide chimney to look normal in size. In fact, it is surprisingly large—spacious enough to contain a stairwell. In the same

way, the second-level windows look small from the outside but are actually a generous 4 ft. tall.

A full stair leads to the third-level loft. This area is tucked under the roof but it remains acoustically open to the level below. The black metal rails have a no-nonsense industrial character.

of depth to all three rooms, making the house seem bigger.

Thad and Sheila wanted a house that would accommodate a number of guests, and the stair continues up to a third-level loft tucked under the roof. There is one window set high in each gable wall, as well as a skylight at the top of the stair tower, ensuring that this area is cheerily illuminated.

To successfully reduce a well-known icon like a gabled house to its elements, an architect needs to pay especially careful attention to proportions. The *pitch* (or angle) of this home's roof is set at 45 degrees. This particular slope has an intuitive logic—it is straightforward and pleasingly familiar. The second-level walls are kept low, giving the bedrooms partially sloped ceilings. The lower walls also help prevent the house from looming too tall, and Geoff Warner wanted to maintain the blocky look that was the initial inspiration for the house.

This home's design succeeds because it is familiar without being a literal copy. The color approximates that of a barn, and the shape is the distillation of a farmhouse. So, even though Thad and Sheila's house is sleek and modern, it pays homage to generations of rural buildings that came before it.

Slanting Silhouette

THE GABLE ROOF IS SO INTIMATELY CONNECTED with the idea of a home that a child's first drawings often include those slanting planes. The particular shape and pitch of the roof help identify the style and era of a house. For example, the low hipped roofs of Prairie-style architecture extend out toward the horizon; the very steep pitch of romantic Gothic cottages reaches up to the heavens; and we associate flat roofs with Modern, cube-like houses.

A gable roof may be picturesque, but it came about for the practical need to shed water and snow away from the sheltered space. A steep gable also has the benefit of creating more living space just below the roof, most often for sleeping and storage. The home shown here has a 45-degree pitch, a traditionally popular slope because it involves simple geometry in the framing of the roof.

This farmhouse is an aggregate of several forms. It avoids looking too busy because the forms are kept simple, with well-ordered windows and a consistent palette of white siding and stone used throughout.

Instant Evolution

PART OF THE ENDURING APPEAL OF FARMHOUSES is that they are seen as having grown older gracefully, with sensible additions made as needed over the years. To build a new house in this general style, an architect can try to create a sense of history—to suggest a story that goes back generations.

Architect Ann Decker designed this Maryland farmhouse as a haphazard collection of forms, so that it gives the impression of having expanded in response to the needs of generations of owners. She went about this in several ways. The roof heights are varied, as is the roofing material itself—from cedar shingles on the steep gables to the stainless-steel standing-seam roof above the front porch. In the same way, the stone cladding is intentionally misaligned between one form and the next. As a result, the house doesn't look like a developer's box but a landmark wedded to its site.

A subtle change in the density of battens distinguishes the main and upper levels. The textures of the siding and metal roof add interest without overwhelming the simple forms.

The stone base of the house has a massive, solid appearance, while the vertical board-and-batten of the upper stories increases the impression of height. Square little windows are tucked between the brackets of the roof's overhang, much in the manner of a barn.

Rural Assembly

At a glance, you can see that this is no slavish re-creation of a rural American icon. The shifts in materials and treatments do more than suggest age. The home takes on remarkably different personalities, depending on the vantage point. From the front, the house seems quite low and modest, rather than proclaiming its presence to the street. The two ends are stepped down from the home's tall center, so that they look like cottages. Circle around to the back, and the structure is now an impressive three stories tall, with lots of glass to take in the view.

Although this house may be something of a chameleon, its faces all share a passing resemblance to a barn. In fact, the structure almost looks as though a vintage barn had been embedded within later framed additions. On the interior, this makes it possible to create spaces of different scale, both intimate and expansive.

While both the color of the house and its open front porch are in the manner of a farmhouse, the board-and-batten siding, galvanized gutters and light fixtures, and straightforward brackets at the overhangs all keep one foot solidly planted in the functional barn aesthetic.

The center of the home is a lofty two-story dining and living space with the openness of a barn—but the resemblance doesn't go much further. Instead of a vaulted roof with hand-hewn timbers, this room has a flat ceiling supported by painted, refined crossbeams. The wide oak planks of the floor are a match for the room's scale. So is

IN DETAIL

Patina

FARMHOUSES HAVE AN ASSOCIATION with materials that develop an attractive weathered look over time—wood siding, shingles, wide-plank floors, and even stone. A honed granite countertop does require some maintenance, unlike polished granite; but the flat finish is less flashy and formal, and its porous nature means that daily use will gradually age the surface into an ever-more subtle material.

At the rear of the house, the intimate cottage-like appearance of the end form gives way to walls of windows. The two wings of the house create a sheltered spot for a deck that is shared by the kitchen and the main living space.

The walls that wrap the window seat reflect light, helping define this alcove as a distinct and separate place in the room. The face and sides of the bench are clad in painted panels of wood for durability and a furniture-like aesthetic.

This bathroom runs through a scale of neutrals, from pale gray walls to the charcoal slate floor to the black granite countertops. The shade can be drawn at the lower window for privacy, leaving the upper transom open for daylight.

the anchoring presence of the fireplace, laid up of the same stone used for the exterior walls.

This area has two tiers of glass that reach high enough for Tom and Carol, the owners, to watch the property's 100-ft.-tall trees swaying in the wind. Four sets of glass French doors lead out to a deck, and when the leaves fall, the doors allow glimpses of the Potomac River in the distance.

A second-level gallery along one side runs above a flagstone path on the first level. The gallery connects the bedrooms at opposite ends of the house, serving as a hall that enjoys views to the outdoors and to the activities in the central living and dining space below.

Intimate Spaces

Set off from the boldly open central space, the one-story kitchen feels like a haven. Its layout is such that the messier half, with the sink and cooktop, is farthest from the living and dining area. The nearest counter has a wide ledge set just above the backsplash to serve as a buffet for the adjacent dining table.

The kitchen's cherry flat-panel cabinets are straightforward, with classic half-round pulls and no fussy frills. Black granite countertops provide a counterpoint to the white painted woodwork found throughout the house. Tom and Carol are both biochemists, and the granite has been

The strong rectilinear shape of the main living space is softened by the second-level gallery to one side and the organic shapes of the stone in the fireplace. The rooms of the house are organized around this central core.

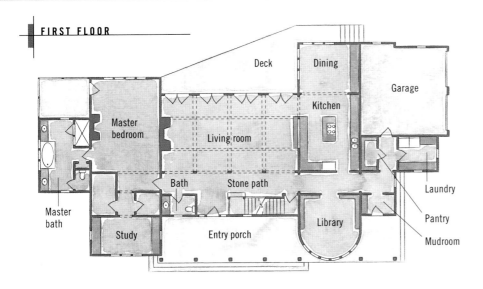

Deck · Dining · Garage · Kitchen · Master bedroom · Living room · Laundry · Master bath · Bath · Stone path · Pantry · Study · Entry porch · Library · Mudroom

honed to the smooth, flat finish of the laboratory benchtops they know so well. An eating area at the end of the kitchen has tall banks of windows on two sides, so that sitting there is like having a picnic in the woods.

The stone path runs past the kitchen and into the pantry, so that this little room can handle the knocks and occasional spills of a vacuum cleaner and wet buckets. Tom and Carol agree they will never have another house without a walk-in pantry.

Just as the exterior of the house has different personalities, the library is an intimate alternative to the central living space. Its interior walls

Oversized thresholds cased with simple flat trim define the transition from kitchen to eating area so that the space does not feel like one long shotgun room.

are wrapped in bookshelves, and a faceted wall of windows noses out from the home. While Tom and Carol liked the idea of having a room with a round shape, they didn't want an ostentatious two-story tower. Ann's solution was to have this curving wall stop at one story and to cap it with the low-pitched shed roof of the front porch. The library's continuous band of windows floods the room with daylight and relieves a side of the house that otherwise has only small punched openings of the sort you'd see on a barn.

The window at the end of the long flagstone hall draws people down the central path through the house. The stones were selected with an eye toward including a variety of tones, from a sandy color that picks up on the adjacent wood floor to charcoal gray and even some purple hues.

The circular shape of the window wall in the sunny library focuses the attention inward for reading or quiet conversation and outward to the view of the hayfield across the street.

The steps off the back deck hug the side of the house and pass through a patch of flowers. The small square windows at the front of the house appear here as transoms above casements.

The sliding barnstyle doors have a glass upper half so that, even when closed, light from within is shared with the hall. The bookshelf cubes have a modern look and yet they also relate to the traditional muntins in the transom windows.

A Hint of Barn, a Whiff of Manure

This home's rural character is underscored by the way in which the surrounding acreage is used. It is located in a "cluster development" in which homeowners built on smaller lots to free up a generous parcel of common land. This preserves a working horse farm and hay fields right in the center of the community—and the neighborhood feels like a *real* community, rather than the typical isolated scattering of suburban houses on 2-acre plots. The meadow across the street from Tom and Carol's home is still actively cultivated, and the occasional whiff of manure at fertilizing time certifies that the land hasn't all gone to weekly mown bluegrass.

At the same time, the house has an edge that preserves it from being quaint in any way. Tom requested that Ann find ways of working an unconventional material into the home—metal, with its association of being used in hardworking

The front porch and large windows in the library make the lower public level of the front facade feel welcoming, while the small windows above suggest the presence of private quarters on the second floor.

outbuildings. Tom was delighted when Ann suggested using panels of chicken wire for the gallery railing; this informal detail helps keep the central living area in the casual spirit of the rest of the house.

Considering how many forms and shapes come together in this house, the result might have seemed a disjointed jumble from the outside. The seemingly obvious selection of white paint for both the siding and trim should not be overlooked. This classic color unifies the house and provides an enduring rural aesthetic. The many forms of the house hold together as an authentic collection that seems to have been accumulating for years.

Bringing the Outdoors In

A SMOOTH TRANSITION between inside and outside helps a house feel grounded in its environment. Carrying a material such as stone or siding between the two can act as a bridge.

In this house, the flagstone used outside on the front porch flows inside the front door to the main circulation path running the length of the house. The fireplace is made of the same Maryland fieldstone as the exterior walls, giving the house an integrity that applied style cannot match. When most traditional farmhouses were constructed, only a limited number of materials were available, and the resulting consistent palette makes them coherent and charming to the eye.

Old Farm, New Farmhouse

L EAVING THE CITY BEHIND, a San Francisco couple was searching Sonoma County for a rural retreat when they discovered a fallow 212-acre farm complete with a walnut orchard, plum trees, and cow barn. The scattering of outbuildings was charming, but the aging farmhouse had to go. It had a decrepit wood foundation and did not structurally meet earthquake codes. Renovation was out of the question, and the owners decided to demolish the structure.

They were determined to create a new house with a timeless character, one that would fit in seamlessly with its supporting cast of outbuildings. Drawing on childhood memories of rural New England, the couple wanted the design to have some of the characteristics of Greek Revival farmhouses. Although this style originated in the East, it is not foreign to California, having traveled to the Pacific Coast with the first westward wave of farmers.

The outbuildings were hardly necessary to their new life, but the owners decided to restore them for the sake of the farm's heritage. They even added one. Their architect, David Gast, was

Nestled in the Mayacamas Mountains, the structures on this farm in Sonoma County create a sense of community. The utilitarian outbuildings have distinctive shapes, sizes, and colors that reflect their history and function.

The shallow porch outside the living room both shades the house from the hot sun in summer months and frames generous views out over the countryside.

inspired by the region's wooden water towers and designed one as a *folly*, a built feature that exists for the fun of it rather than to serve a practical purpose. (The tower is actually hooked up to the farm's water supply and provides water pressure during the area's occasional power outages.) Together, the vertical water tower, a long four-car garage, and the gabled house sit like three old friends having a good conversation around the dinner table.

As with farmhouses of the past, this one has a gracious front porch to welcome visitors, and the porch's northern orientation makes it a cool place to relax on hot summer days—on either of two levels, because the flat roof serves as a balcony. A second porch wraps around the south side of the house. Part of its length is screened in for outdoor dining safe from the ever-present hornets.

Down-Home Greek Revival

After the United States gained independence from Great Britain, the culture of ancient Greece became an important influence on the new nation because it symbolized democracy. The Greek Revival style, loosely based on Greek temples, was popular for a time, spreading from east to west and appealing to many American farmers along the way. Some of the hallmarks of a Greek Revival house are shown here.

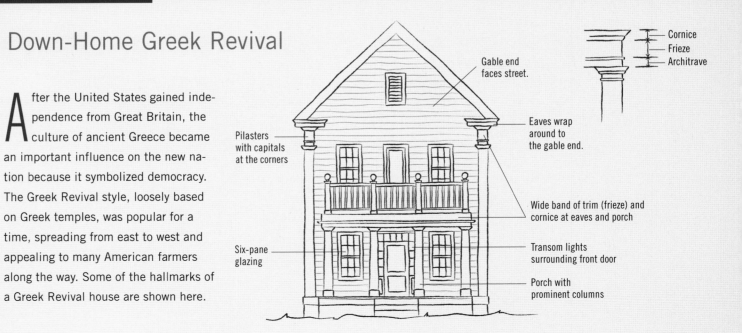

Gable end faces street.

Cornice
Frieze
Architrave

Pilasters with capitals at the corners

Eaves wrap around to the gable end.

Wide band of trim (frieze) and cornice at eaves and porch

Six-pane glazing

Transom lights surrounding front door

Porch with prominent columns

A drawback of deep, wide porches is that they can make the home seem dark. Skylights in the roof of this porch bring daylight into the rooms within.

Extending the entire length of the home, the back porch creates a flowing transition between inside and out. Oversized steps further blend home with yard.

SITE PLAN

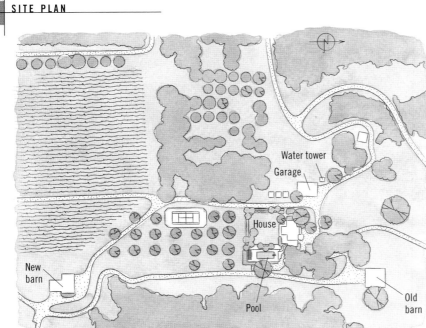

Water tower

Garage

House

New barn

Pool

Old barn

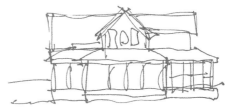

California Greek

David's design fits in so well that the new farmhouse is often mistaken for a renovation. The two-story center of the home incorporates the traditional features of Greek Revival, with the classical columns and details one might expect. In contrast, the wings appear to have been added later. This effectively helps break down the scale of the house and makes it look as though it has always been the centerpiece of this old farmstead.

The interiors also have a traditional feel, with their paneled walls, chair rail, cove moldings, and historic colors. In this updated version of a vintage layout, there are clear boundaries but open visual connections between the public living spaces. The view from the formal front entry sweeps all the way through the house, past

The welcoming front porch softens the formal symmetry of this tall, stately farmhouse. Its second-level deck is reached from a door in the front bedroom.

The exterior lines of the home's wings are kept clean by tucking two second-level porches into the roof.

the stair hall, and into the living room. In the living room, the eye is drawn to windows on three sides and French doors leading to the open porch. And in one wing of the home, the kitchen and dining room are visually connected yet separated by a pair of counters and upper cabinets with glass doors. A study and guest suite occupy the other wing; these rooms could become a main-level master suite as the owners age.

In this house, the hardworking service areas—the mudroom, laundry room, pantry, and bathroom—are located behind a door beyond the kitchen. Unlike suburban mudrooms used

Only time can create the gracious patina of old age. But careful detailing and thoughtful use of new and recycled materials can ease the sharp edges of new construction.

The distinctive eaves are trimmed classically, in traditional Greek Revival fashion. Farmhouses continued to be built in this style for years after it ceased to be popular in America's urban areas.

The living room's boundary is distinguished from the adjacent stair hall by the use of a beam and column, waist-high cabinetry, and a subtle change in the direction of the floorboards.

Cleanup after a day in the fields requires a dedicated room, not just a hallway. The durable floor in this mudroom is Pennsylvania bluestone—a connection back to the homeowners' eastern roots.

for social calendars, sorting mail, and answering phone messages, the one in this house is truly a room for mud. The orchard still requires maintenance and the homeowners get their hands dirty mowing, pruning, and gardening.

Paneling with Plum Stakes

The owners took pleasure in finding treasures amid the hand-me-down junk inherited with the property. The stove from the original house warms the mudroom. Wooden stakes that held up branches ripe with plums now panel the walls of the study. Cabinet tops in the living and dining rooms are made of walnut harvested from trees on the site. Taking cues from the old farmhouse, David clad the kitchen with a tongue-and-groove ceiling and included a walk-in pantry. The wood floors throughout the main level are larch, a regional deciduous conifer with a fine grain and even coloration similar to Douglas fir. In these ways, the home is tied to both its location and its history.

Through many seasons, the couple had lived with the perpetual fog that tempers the weather in San Francisco Bay, and by contrast they wanted their second home to embrace both the heat of summer and the crisp clear air of autumn. When the doors on the north and south sides of the house are open, the breezes blow right through for natural air-conditioning. The main floor has easy access to the outdoors, with just two steps separating the porches from the yard—a refreshing change from unavoidable flights of stairs in San Francisco.

On beautiful nights, occupants of the second-floor bedrooms can enjoy the breeze—each bedroom has its own private porch. The porches are recessed into the roof pitch to keep from cluttering the lines of the home and to give a sheltered, contained feeling that an open balcony wouldn't offer.

The plentiful porches, upstairs and down, help set the tone for this farmhouse, reinforcing its role as a retreat from the routines of urban life. The kitchen also makes the owners' intent

Defined by pilasters and columns, thresholds mark the transition between entry, stair hall, and living room, and yet there is a clear view through the house. A skylight in the stair hall keeps this centrally located space full of light.

When the French doors are opened in this bedroom, the space effectively becomes a sleeping porch, admitting country scents and sounds. Double screen doors help keep nature at bay.

clear. It isn't designed to heat up the quick-prep meals of a busy weekday life but has room for multiple cooks to craft meals that simmer and brew all day long. As with many farmhouses, the porches and kitchen are the defining elements.

This California farmstead evolved from a place of hard work and economic livelihood in previous generations to a peaceful retreat for a modern, urban family. The graceful new farmhouse fits seamlessly in the center of the old farmstead, rejuvenating the place for years to come.

Traditional trim, including frame-and-panel doors and paneling, brings the interiors back to the mid-1800s.

With a kitchen island the size of a dining table, there's room enough for the entire family to assemble for informal meals. The wood countertop is welcoming to leaning elbows.

A Porch Primer

A GOOD PORCH IS AN INTEGRAL PART of the overall design of a house—a farmhouse in particular. The considerations include size, roof configuration, relationship to the ground, proportions, and style.

For a front porch, a depth of 6 ft. or 7 ft. provides a gracious space, large enough for guests waiting at the front door or for sitting socially. Expanding the depth up to 10 ft. makes it possible to accommodate a dining table or sofa. The pitch of the roof is typically shallower than that of the house itself to allow generous windows on the second floor. On a deep porch, a flat roof avoids this problem and also offers the opportunity for a second-floor balcony.

A porch can look stable and balanced, sleek and light, or grounded and heavy, depending on the proportions of its columns. The substantial columns on this Greek Revival farmhouse emphasize the style's characteristic monumentality.

In most parts of the country, if the floor of a porch is more than 30 in. off the ground, a 3-ft.-high guard rail is required by Code. This railing can be a design asset or liability, depending on the character of the house. If you want to maintain an open feeling and emphasize the home's vertical proportions, keep the porch low to the ground and omit the railing.

As you approach the
house, its carefully
arranged symmetry and
balance become evident.
The three distinct parts—
house, garage, and the
link between them—are
visually related through
the use of like materials.

In the Image of a Barn

NOSTALGIA IS A GOOD STARTING POINT for design. For the
owners of this house in the rolling hills of Connecticut,
it was memories of an old barn that struck a chord. The
structure belonged to one of the owners' grandparents, who converted it into a summer-only living room. With an exposed two-story
timber frame, it served as a dramatic space for family gatherings.

When the couple purchased a meadow bordered on two sides
by woods, they decided to re-create something of the old barn's
heft and atmosphere. Both are architects, and they sat down at
their drawing boards to sketch initial ideas. Intriguingly, both of
them came up with the notion of arranging the house and garage
to form an exterior courtyard. Their final design blends a timber
frame reminiscent of the grandfather's barn with a courtyard, and
it does so with symmetry, good proportions, and a simple color
palette of white paint.

Seen from a distance, the simple forms of the house and
garage resemble New England barns—or even children's
blocks tossed down upon the landscape.

The gabled link is an in-between space that feels like it's half inside and half outside. It leads to a set of French doors, establishing them as the main, everyday entry to the home.

Unadorned Simplicity

As visitors approach the property, the gabled facades of the house and garage stand attentively on the crest of a hill as if surveying the adjacent fields. The two buildings are connected by a one-story link. Their order and symmetry have an overall look of spareness that is characteristic of barns. You might think you've come upon a pair of outbuildings because of the simplicity: no

overhangs, no porches, no decorative detailing, no artful variation in color. Up close, however, there are signs of domestication, such as the well-kept courtyard, a spindle-backed bench, stacked firewood, French doors, and an abundance of windows.

The house is clearly a house. And yet as you step inside, it again feels as though you've encountered a barn—a glance to either side might reveal hay lofts and barn owls. The heavy timber frame overhead encourages you to take a deep breath and stride out into a refreshingly airy room. At the same time, the area is obviously devoted to dining and living sections. The timber structure helps define these spaces.

The size of the living room's wide center *bay*, or section of framing, was determined by the couple's intention to use an old carpet from the grandfather's barn. The carpet, along with the intervals of posts and beams, serves as an indication of the room's boundaries. The dining room table sits comfortably within one smaller bay, and a game table occupies the other. The bays also define two 7-ft.-wide side aisles for circulation running the length of the three central spaces.

At dusk, the glowing windows and doors highlight the regular rhythm of the home's composition. If the design intent for the exterior form and for the interior spaces are not in harmony, this careful alignment might easily be sacrificed, resulting in a less sophisticated house.

The understated walls seem to disappear, allowing the frame to define the living areas within the home. Walls of bookshelves establish opposite ends of the space on the first floor and add texture to the otherwise smooth interior surfaces.

With its lower ceiling, a one-story area within the central open space establishes a pathway between the kitchen and the guest bedrooms. Above this ceiling, a gallery ties together the two lofts.

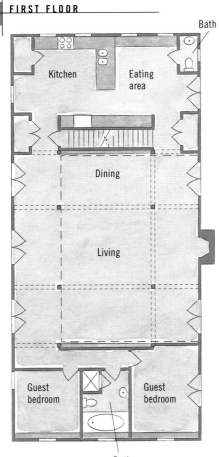

FIRST FLOOR

A repetition of parts contributes to the home's overall sense of calm and simplicity. The living space is divided by the timber frame into three structural bays, each with centrally placed French doors and upper windows.

The frame seems to have always been there, like an old skeleton with a new skin. Its cross-beams, set at 9 ft. above the floor, give human scale to a space that could otherwise feel overwhelmingly large. Unlike traditional barns, the rafters overhead are concealed within the insulated roof; only the posts and beams are exposed. The result is a marked contrast between the massive wood frame and clean, unadorned drywall.

A Courtyard Within

Just as the walls of the house and garage shape the exterior courtyard, opposing walls of floor-to-ceiling bookshelves create the effect of an interior courtyard. These shelves somewhat resemble walls of dry-stacked stone. Above them, the second-level master bedroom and study are visible as open lofts, with views back down through the timber frame.

To preserve the openness of the main barn-like space, the kitchen and the guest bedrooms and bath are tucked at opposite ends of the house. The kitchen provides a more intimate gathering space than the lofty central courtyard. This room is bright and open in plan, divided between a working kitchen and an eating area that

A utility closet was placed so that it defines a break between the expansive living room and the more intimate kitchen. The 8-ft.-tall French doors suit the scale of the vaulted living room, while standard 6-ft., 8-in. doors are used for the closet.

Balanced Symmetry

BOTH OUTSIDE AND IN, this house is a study of symmetry and balance. Solid forms are played against open spaces, or *voids* in architect-speak. This pattern of solid–void–solid is used in symmetrical compositions throughout the house; the consistent ordering creates an underlying stability and predictability. The result is a home that feels serene and balanced—yet not at all static or boring, because this pattern is used at different scales and in different ways.

The house itself is formed by two similarly shaped buildings—the house and garage—separated by the void of the courtyard. Inside, the main two-story living space is book-ended by two solids, one containing the kitchen with bedroom loft above and the other the guest bedrooms with study above. This pattern

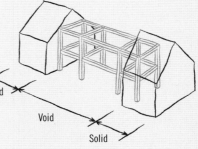

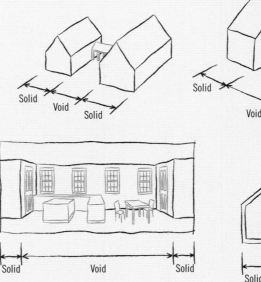

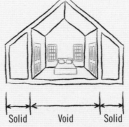

works on a smaller scale, too: In the kitchen, the open working and eating space is flanked by the pantry on one side and the powder room on the other; similarly, the loft-like openness of the master bedroom is contained by the forms of a closet and a bathroom.

The gallery runs between the lofts for the master bedroom and studio. It takes advantage of the ceiling's low slope to provide still more shelving for the couple's books.

With careful forethought, a low ceiling can give rooms an attractive snugness. In this second-floor bathroom, the toilet and tub are tucked underneath the roof. The partial timber frame at the ceiling's vault visually connects the bathroom to the central living space.

The bathroom's open, airy, barnlike ambiance is maintained by providing a vintage armoire for linens and toiletries, along with a freestanding sink. An interior window shares light from the shower skylight with the stairwell below.

As seen across the main living space from the study, the timber frame outlines the master bedroom loft. The heavy frame stands in contrast to the unadorned walls and ceiling planes.

doubles as a workspace for correspondence and sorting mail. A walk-in pantry and plenty of cabinets make it possible to have large windows just above the kitchen counters, flooding the room with daylight. A set of French doors gives ready access to a terrace for outdoor meals.

A thick, low stone wall surrounds the terrace, forming a boundary while allowing an open view of the distant fields and woods. The south-facing orientation extends the outdoor season from early spring to late fall. The opposite side of the house provides a very different kind of outdoor space—its courtyard is inward focused, protected, and private. During the warmer months, sets of French doors on both sides of the main living

space can be flung open, turning the entire house into a breezy screen porch.

The design successfully incorporates aspects of a home with the unapologetic directness of a barn. As with the front door to the house, interior details are purposefully de-emphasized. It wouldn't seem out of place to see a ladder leaning up against the old timbers—especially since the stairway happens to be hidden between one wall of books and another of kitchen cabinets. The baseboards and window trim consist of a plain, flat board, painted the same color as the walls to keep the eye on the overall design rather than drawing attention to the detailing. In the same way, the fireplace is completely devoid of

Generously sized double-hung windows provide more than adequate daylight to display treasured collections. The view out the window is as trim and composed as the arrangement of furniture and artifacts within.

millwork—there is simply a firebox set in the wall. The orange flames and two wingback chairs (rescued from the old barn) are all the ornament that is needed there.

Considerable thought was given to providing ample storage in a way that would preserve the home's airy feeling. Closets run along exterior walls and are strategically placed in transition areas between major living spaces.

When a design begins with a memory, it can involve the transfer of ideas between generations and across building types—in this case, from grandfather to granddaughter and from barn to house. For this couple, their home was instantly familiar. The final design is a bridge from the past.

All White

This house is unabashedly white, inside and out. This may seem like an easy, bland color scheme, but a distinctive design can look particularly elegant in white. White lets the forms, shadows, proportions, and—in this case—the frame become the eye catchers.

From a distance, the exterior of this house looks flat and white, with little to distract attention from the handsome form. As you approach, however, both the vertical lines of the flush-board siding and the wood grain become discernable through the solid-white stain. (Unlike paint, stain penetrates the wood and allows the grain to show through.) The subtle texture softens the stark forms of the house. On the inside, the all-white scheme (actually a mix of one half linen paint to one half white paint) is a blank page for the lines of the dramatic timber frame.

The kitchen is a bright, cheery place—and quite efficient. The arrangement of storage spaces, large and small, gives the room a purposeful look. A central counter divides this end of the house into kitchen and eating areas.

A Three-in-One Farmhouse

Pavement has its place, but not around a rustic farmhouse. The three small houses making up this home are connected by paths of limestone, and the gravel driveway not only looks appropriate but also reduces the amount of runoff in heavy rains.

AT FIRST GLANCE, this property in Texas's hill country wasn't all that promising. A tally of its assets included three abandoned stone buildings, two overgrown farm fields, and natural springs trickling nearby. These features might not have been selling points for other buyers, but the new owners-to-be were drawn to the natural beauty of the site and felt a strong sense of welcome and belonging.

With today's high labor costs for construction and comparatively inexpensive materials, the temptation is often to simply clear a property of its tired buildings and start from scratch. But in line with their interest in nature conservancy, the owners took it as their mission to keep the farm intact. They learned that the original settlers were Alsatian, from a region in France that borders Germany, and that the buildings' craftsmanship and simple form may have been influenced by French farmhouses. The couple also wanted to maintain ties to local history. It is likely that all three structures originally belonged to one extended family, who placed the little buildings close together for easy access to a spring and for protection from Native Americans.

The kitchen house and guesthouse look out on a terraced courtyard with a large sheltering tree and wading pond. The spring-fed stream winds through the property in a stone-lined course.

The stark but elegant simplicity of the houses is a clue to their age. Windows and doors were spaced sparingly to save labor, conserve heat, and reduce expenses. With this in mind, the openings in the stone walls have been left few and small, in line with tradition.

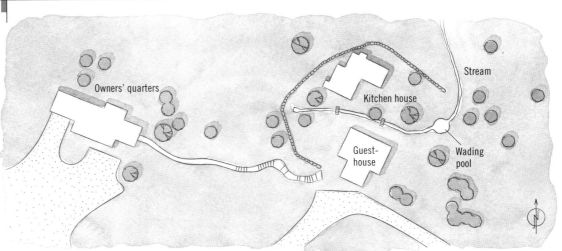

Owners' quarters

Kitchen house

Stream

Guest-house

Wading pool

Stonewalling

THESE HOUSES WERE CON-STRUCTED in the early 1800s, when labor was relatively inexpensive and the area's indigenous limestone could be quarried more affordably than lumber could be sawn. To ensure that new stone added to the project would blend with the old, it was cut with a handheld diamond saw and then distressed with a hatchet to mimic the original texture. The mortar was mixed to nearly match the stone, as on the original walls, creating a monolithic look. But not all definition was lost; the wet mortar was rubbed with a burlap bag to slightly recess the pointing and reveal the individual stones.

Up north, stone farmhouses are often remodeled to include insulated interior walls so that winters are more comfortable. But the more moderate climate allowed the owners of this home to leave the stone on the interior wall surface exposed as well.

The property takes much of its character from the abundant presence of water. The road to the ranch skirts the edge of a creek lined with live oaks, sycamores, and cypress. One of the original springs was discovered long ago, when a farmer was digging a pit in which to store potatoes. This spring now supplies the rill running through the courtyard.

Respectful Renovation

Architect William McDonald helped decide how new rooms could be formed within the three separate structures. A building set apart on a small rise is now the owners' quarters, with its two original rooms used as a bedroom and living space. A new screen porch runs along one side, and a board-and-batten addition on the other side holds a small kitchen, mudroom with bath, and carport. This building can work independently if needed.

Down a path of limestone slab steps, a stone retaining wall carves out a level area from the hillside. Here, the guesthouse and kitchen house sit on opposite sides of the small spring-fed stream, which flows down to a stone wading pool and continues a short distance to the creek. For those not up to the jump, large stone slabs span the stream to form a natural-looking bridge between these two buildings. The sheltering canopy of a large tree unifies the whole court-yard, emphasizing its role as the heart of this old ranch.

The kitchen house is the home's main gathering place. The original stone building was too small to contain all the accouterments of a modern kitchen and dining room. So a shed-roofed addition was placed off the back to provide space for the sink, dishwasher, refrigerator, and freezer, with a half-bath tucked at one end. The focal point of the old building is the stove with its

A large slab of limestone bridges the stream on the path between the kitchen-house porch and the guesthouse. Windows in the gable end of the dining room serve to high-light the exposed juniper trusses within.

dramatic copper hood centered on the gable end. Above and below the countertops, open shelves leave the stone walls exposed. The dining room is a large airy porch, open to the elements on three sides but protected by screens. A fireplace anchors the room and serves to add heat and light on cool evenings.

Although this house is in three pieces, they add up to a single coherent home because of the consistent way in which the buildings were renovated. Each gabled stone structure has its copper roof and airy screen porch, and together they create an intimate compound.

KITCHEN HOUSE: FLOOR PLAN

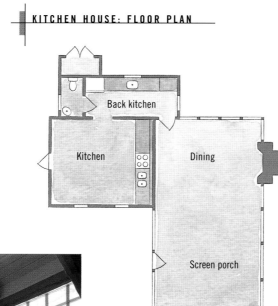

Back kitchen

Kitchen

Dining

Screen porch

The old stone buildings had only a few small windows, by today's standards. The architect left these simple openings unaltered, and brought in daylight by placing clerestory windows in the new shed dormers above. The light from these windows reflects off the ceiling and illuminates the whole room.

The screen porch serves as an alternate dining and living room, and the owners find it to be a refreshing change from the climate-controlled spaces of the city.

As with the other buildings, a generous porch was added to the guesthouse; the visual lightness of the porch has a wonderful yin–yang relationship with the solid-stone walls. The guest bedroom and sitting area occupy the central space of the house, and the mudroom, bathroom, and dressing room face the courtyard, where they are easily accessible after a dip in the wading pool or creek.

Although the home was not meant to be an authentic restoration of pioneer architecture, the design retains its historical roots. The three old buildings clearly remain the anchors of the site, with additions enhancing but not overwhelming them. New shed dormers are well proportioned, and they pop up just enough to let in daylight through clerestory windows. The limestone walls were tuck pointed to keep them sound for another century, and new masonry was taken from a local quarry for a good match.

The architect kept the original window and door openings, a decision that helped organize the arrangement of new rooms while lending an endearing quirkiness to the home. For example, the new screen porch off the guesthouse is reached by two separate doors just 4 ft. apart— a reminder to visitors that this building had a former life.

Material Evidence

The three buildings are clearly tied together by a consistent palette of materials, colors, and details. Exposed trusses, made of local juniper, support new standing-seam copper roofs. The tongue-and-groove decking on the ceilings is stained a creamy shade that matches the stone; the choice of a light color keeps the interior open and airy while highlighting the wood trusses.

The wood-burning fireplace in the dining porch takes the edge off of cool mornings and evenings while providing a focal point for the room all year long. The exposed trusses of the intersecting gables create an intriguing web overhead.

All three porches are built on low stone walls. The walls create a sense of protective enclosure and tie the porches visually to the original stone houses. They also have the practical function of keeping the wood framing off the ground so that it is less vulnerable to termites and moisture.

Floors in the high-traffic spaces are of concrete, stained and sealed and then waxed for a finished appearance. All the bedrooms have warmer, more forgiving floors of pine.

The trio of little houses now seem to be members of the extended family. The owners talk about them as though they are dear relatives, each with its subtle differences in stonework, views, and history.

This multibuilding approach is often an option for older farm properties. It may be more trouble to maintain individual structures, but these owners find that their lives are better integrated with the natural world than if they lived in a conventional home. The spaces between the buildings function as outdoor rooms or hallways, with leafy roofs, fresh breezes, and full-moon night-lights.

While it may have been the couple's sixth sense about the place that sold them on the

Grounded in the Past

Indigenous materials are typically used throughout early homesteads, inherently tying them to the surrounding landscape. The architect and owners of this Texas home were careful to respectfully leave clues to the past in the new design.

The original stonework received particular attention. Although the owners' quarters had been built of refined-looking dressed stone, the other two houses were cobbled together with recycled

stone from an earlier structure, rubble from the site, and even surplus adobe bricks. The existing window and door openings in the stone walls were maintained; their positions helped define room layouts, and their proportions are essential to maintaining the charm of these traditional houses.

Smaller details count, as well. The wooden pegs once used to anchor the original window frames have been left imbedded in the stone, surrounding the

openings in a decorative way. And outside the kitchen house, the remains of an old stone smokehouse sit untouched as a mysterious ruin.

property, the old ranch is a feast for the other senses as well. This is a place of quiet, where only the sounds of the natural spring, birdsong, and good conversation have license to break the silence. Even the air smells fresher, because of the site's elevation. And the buttery-colored limestone, still bearing the markings of the mason, lends its distinctly mellowed character to the setting, as if the buildings were pulled right up out of the surrounding earth.

The bathroom walls stop short of the ceiling, allowing an uninterrupted row of transom windows above. An interior wall was framed to create a handy ledge above the wall-mounted faucet and to conceal the plumbing.

OWNERS' QUARTERS: FLOOR PLAN

Garage

Carport

Kitchen

Bath

Bedroom

Living

Screen porch

GUESTHOUSE: FLOOR PLAN

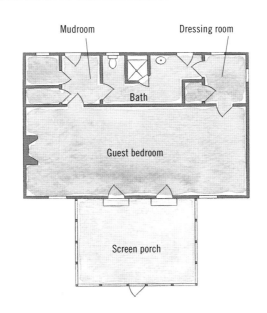

Mudroom

Dressing room

Bath

Guest bedroom

Screen porch

The trusses are made of juniper, a wood indigenous to the area. It is highly durable—resistant to rot and unappealing to termites. The bark was removed with a high-powered water spray, revealing canoe-shaped veins that add a distinctive fluidity to the wood.

This house is composed of traditional forms that have been assembled in a modern way. The triangular dormers repeat the shape of the gable-end walls on a smaller scale.

Farmhouse with an Edge

As LINDA AND STEVE SEARCHED THROUGH BOOKS and magazines for ideas on what their new farmhouse might look like, they found inspiration in the simple geometric forms of Modern architecture. In particular, they were drawn to homes that were "deconstructed" into pieces—much like the clustered appearance of a traditional farmstead. They determined that one of the pieces would have the distinctive round shape of a silo. Another basic decision was that the house would be on one level, allowing them to grow old in it. The couple also saw their home as having lots of blank wall planes on which bold patterns of light and shadow would be cast.

Architect Reeves Weideman took the project from there, designing a house that captures the farmhouse spirit in a modern way.

Sculpture in the Landscape

The site had an old barn in a hollow not far from the entrance gate, but Linda and Steve decided to place the house a half mile away on the top of a knoll. From there, five fingers of pasture radiate out for the open views that initially inspired the move from the city. As

The owners have left the base of the building devoid of landscaping so that their home looks like a sculptural object placed on the land.

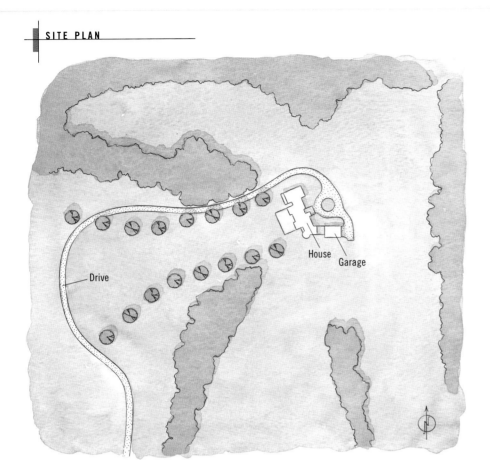

Drive

House
Garage

for the barn area, there is now an organic garden, screen porch, and horse stable, creating a second focal point for the farm.

This intentional separation between barnyard and house ensures that the couple actively experiences the entire property rather than just one corner of it. And because they spend as much time outside as in, it matters a good deal that their house functions as a well-placed piece of sculpture in the landscape. In keeping with their original vision, the structure is simply set on an open plane with a crisp roofline against an intense blue sky; they have not added foundation plantings or trees around the house because traditional landscaping might detract from the design, and decks are kept low to the ground for the same reason.

When siting a house, an outstanding view may override other, more practical considerations. With this project, Reeves oriented the house with a window wall that faces west to catch a view. He

Playful and Practical

The American farm has evolved a number of distinctive structures that are no longer strictly needed on a modern homestead but continue to serve as rural icons. Architects draw inspiration from red barns, white farmhouses, slatted corncribs—and silos.

The silo is instantly recognizable and can be incorporated with a new farmhouse in a playful way. This farmhouse interprets the silo as a round structure located at the hinge point between two wings. It is not as tall as its authentic precedents—the interior would have been intimidatingly high and difficult to put to good use.

Inside, the round two-story space is used as an office. Outside, it is clad in red shakes, further distinguishing its form from the white horizontal clapboard siding. And its verticality helps visually pin the house to the hill.

then extended a deep overhang to mitigate the full exposure to the heat of the afternoon sun.

As visitors approach, the house comes in to view as geometric blocks—two white gabled forms and a red silo, all floating in the sea of grass under a dome of sky. Curtain walls of glass virtually disappear at the home's connecting links, emphasizing the sense of four separate buildings while maintaining the convenience of a single dwelling. There are also traditional elements in the design: the simple symmetry of the white clapboard gables, the silo, and cross-buck boards on the garage doors. Although some windows have muntins, Reeves ganged and stacked the units in untraditional configurations. As with many farmhouses, this one has dormers, but they are unusual—crisply geometric triangles filled with glass. A hovering cantilevered roof shelters the front door and deck. There are no classic front porch posts here.

The texture of the white-on-white clapboard siding and cross-buck door is highlighted by shadows as the sun moves across the sky. As on a barn, the large sliding door provides convenient access to the back of the extra-deep garage.

Two tall chimney stacks divide the large living space into the living room, dining room, and kitchen. The spare decor of the house is by design: The owners plan to add art slowly to avoid ending up with a cluttered look.

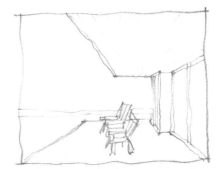

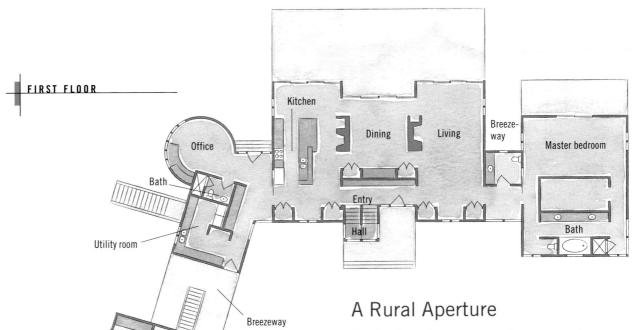

Sliding glass doors open the dining room up to the waving prairie outside. The symmetry of the room is challenged by a tall slit of ribbed glass in the alcove, sharing light with the front entry just beyond the wall.

A Rural Aperture

Inside, the only suggestion that you are in a farmhouse is the view to the fields. And the view is the centerpiece of the home. As you enter, the eye is drawn to the landscape beyond the western glass wall shared by the living room, dining room, and kitchen. The spare, white interior sets off the vibrant colors and textures of the fields, making an ever-changing mural of the meadow's restored grasses.

The kitchen and living room anchor the ends of the vaulted space, and a pair of freestanding chimney stacks define the dining room in the center. The long island in the galley kitchen has a high ledge that serves to hide the sink at one end and an extended countertop for stools at the other end (see the photo on p. 95). The walnut base and granite top give the island a furniture-like feel, while the white cabinets blend in with the walls. Across from the island, a fireplace is at counter height so that it can be enjoyed by someone preparing meals. A nook for wood storage is conveniently placed just below. Modern details help maintain the minimal aesthetic—flush-face cabinets, fireplaces surrounded by stainless steel or blackened steel plates, and walls without the usual baseboard trim.

Instead of having a kitchen table, the owners chose to create a comfortable hangout spot. The exterior wall steps in to help define this nook within the open, free-flowing space.

The deck's deep overhang provides shelter from the sun on the treeless crest of the field. The cantilevered roof means there are no posts to interrupt the long dramatic view. The striations of the deck boards and ribbed galvanized soffits both echo the flat horizon line.

A cantilevered roof extends out, shading the curtain wall of glass and sheltering a deck. Linda and Steve have avoided the temptation to fill the deck with pots and a lot of furniture, opting instead for only a handful of simple deck chairs lined up to look out over the waving prairie.

From the kitchen, a hallway leads to a round office in the silo. A tall bank of windows makes the office an ideal place to view the moon; aside from writing checks and stargazing, Linda and

Connected Cluster

A RURAL SITE SEEMS TO CRY OUT for a cluster of buildings rather than a lone house, perhaps because it provides a sense of security. The owners of this new farmhouse chose a design that links together four forms—the garage, home office silo, main living space, and master bedroom. The roof ties together these elements, while the wall surface is interrupted by floor-to-ceiling areas of glass

that read as dark voids. With a similar effect, a covered open-air deck creates a break between garage and house. The result is a house that suggests a settlement instead of looking like an isolated, monolithic structure imposed on the landscape.

Steve find that the room's couch is the best spot in the house for a nap.

Storage Plays a Supporting Role

The generous utility room and back hall make the home's spare aesthetic possible by providing plenty of storage in which to keep things out of sight. This is the catchall drop zone for Linda and Steve as they walk from garage to kitchen, sparing the rest of the house from clutter. The utility room has a sink for arranging flowers from the garden and even a second dishwasher for vases and overflow dinner dishes.

In the open-air link to the garage, a galvanized-steel stair leads to a second-floor guest room. While this bedroom is actually detached from the house, the master suite at the other end is removed from the living space by one of the glassy links. The suite has a vaulted ceiling, open to

A hallway doesn't have to be a corridor pinched between parallel walls. This circulation path passes through the kitchen, front foyer, and living room on its way to the master bedroom. A day-lit wall is a focal point at the end of the path.

The tall, vaulted ceiling of the kitchen is accented by two high windows, one a modern triangular opening in a dormer and the other a traditional rectangle with muntins in the gable end. At the same time, hanging lights help tame the soaring space.

Instead of having a closed closet in the back entry, a pair of side walls extend out to create a niche. Hanging jackets and hats make an artful composition against the crisp white walls. In this house, the painted white baseboard is set in the same plane as the drywall and then defined by a simple reveal where the two materials meet.

Even the open-air link between garage and house received careful attention. The metal stair to the guest quarters has the no-nonsense look of a hay bale conveyor.

As with the main living space, the master bedroom wing is an open area divided into three interrelated parts: bedroom, closet, and bathroom. The long floating vanity counter is tied visually to the shelf in the front entry.

The home's simple symmetry and order reflect both the modern sophistication of the city and the rural vernacular tradition. Each day can begin and end with a view of the landscape that first drew the couple to this site.

large windows in the gables. Interior windows help share light and air between the rooms in the wing. Instead of providing the shade of an overhang, Reeves called for slatted barn doors that can be slid shut to filter the afternoon light.

Even after three years, many of the walls are still bare. Linda and Steve applied the advice of a neighboring farmer to decorating: "If you're not sure, don't do anything. An answer will come in time." And the plain walls have a magic of their own. At certain times of the day, Linda says, the whole house turns pink inside, and she feels as though she were living in the middle of a painting.

Surrounded by mature trees and restored prairie grasses, the new farmhouse looks as if it must have been a renovation. The property does not have a barn but the shingle roof incorporates the red color that is traditionally part of a farm.

New Plot, Old Story

SIX YEARS AGO, Tim phoned his wife, Susan, from a grazing pasture in west central Minnesota with a loaded question: "Do you trust me?" Tim and a real estate agent had just stomped around a 40-acre site and agreed that the land would sell the minute it hit the market. After looking at dozens of properties, Tim was certain that this one had the right stuff—rolling hills, woods, and wetlands all in a rural setting. Susan's answer was yes.

Fitting House to Land

Tim, Susan, and their son, Matthew, were in no hurry to build and move to the new site. They started with a patient restoration of the property. Susan took classes in landscape design to help guide the process, and they called in a team of experts, including people from the U.S. Fish and Wildlife Service, the county conservation district, and the state department of natural resources. The couple learned that their property originally was a cross between upland savannas and North Woods, and they planted more than 700 trees,

This house stands tall above a field of restored prairie grasses. It is located on a rise, as was traditional for farm-houses; this setting, along with the grove of old trees, helps disguise the fact that the house was recently built.

Claiming vs. Merging

WHEN THE OWNERS considered where to put a home in the broad expanse of their land, Dale Mulfinger, one of their architects, asked, "Should the house merge with the land or claim the land?" This choice is explored in the influential book *The Place of Houses,* by Charles Moore, Gerald Allen, and Donlyn Lyndon (Holt, Rinehart & Winston, 1974).

Houses that *merge* with the landscape take cues from the shapes and colors of their natural environment. Think of a cottage in the woods with a steeply pitched roof and textured siding, tucked in with the tall trunks and foliage of surrounding trees. Or consider how the low-pitch hipped roof of a Frank Lloyd Wright Prairie-style house becomes part of the horizon.

Houses that *claim* the land stand in strong contrast to the landscape, even dominating the site. For example, the vertical proportions, steeply pitched roofs, and stark white color of classic Midwestern farmhouses stand out on the horizontal prairie. These qualities serve as symbols of conquering the wilderness and establishing civil order. Typically set on the highest point amid miles of open fields, the houses would have been secure beacons for farmers out working in the fields. Tim and Susan chose this approach, and it was a decision that set the tone for the style and colors of their house.

SITE PLAN

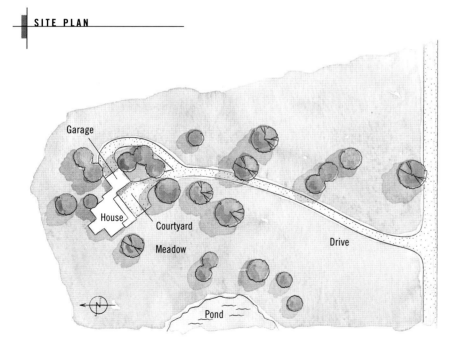

Garage

House

Courtyard

Meadow

Drive

N

Pond

along with native wildflowers and grasses, to reestablish the probable balance that once characterized the area.

As Tim and Susan drew up a *program,* or list of spaces, with architect Paul Buum, it became apparent that the couple's wishes would require a relatively large footprint for a farmhouse. Paul's answer was to design the house in such a way that it appeared to have been expanded with additions over the years. This historical narrative begins with the central form—the "old" gabled farmhouse, done in a weathered-looking, stone-colored stucco with matching windows and trim. The "additions" to each side have fieldstone foundations with a combination of painted white clapboard siding below and board-and-batten siding on the gable ends above. Subtle shifts in the pitch of the roof and style of the windows reinforce the historical plot, while a red roof unifies the whole.

Approaching the house, visitors come to an informal courtyard captured in the elbow created by the house and garage. The home's front facade is given order by a single oversized porch column, centered below the peak of the asymmetrical gable. You might expect to find the front door in this prominent location, but it has been set to one side behind a waist-high stone wall to allow a gracious measure of separation from the public drive.

The house and garage are arranged to form a casual courtyard. The garage doors are recessed, making them less prominent and allowing a sheltered side door entry into the mudroom.

The shed dormer on the garage animates the roofline while expanding the headroom and bringing in daylight for a second-level office.

With its two sections, one open and the other screened, the front porch gets a lot of use. Often a screen porch is relegated to the side or back of the house because it is considered casual, but here it makes the entrance to the home laid-back and inviting.

The bench nook in the vaulted entry foyer is a room within the room. It is defined by V-groove wall paneling and a wood transom overhead. The nook even has an intimate window at just the right height for kids (or dogs) to see who is stepping onto the porch.

A Well-Framed Welcome

The foyer is a generous space that's situated so the heart of the house remains out of sight and quite private. The vaulted ceiling and surrounding overlooks make this feel like a small interior courtyard. For greetings and farewells from the second floor, there is a balcony landing and a bedroom with interior windows. And petite, playful windows, visible when walking up to the house, cast a scattered constellation of sunlight across the wall.

The home's main gathering space is set two steps down from the foyer to give it more height and to reinforce the transition between the two spaces. A beamed ceiling unites the one large room that holds both a dining area and a sitting area with a fireplace and entertainment center. The end wall of this room is all windows with transoms—a departure from farmhouse style, but these windows, although large, have traditional-looking mullions and muntins.

A House of Accretion

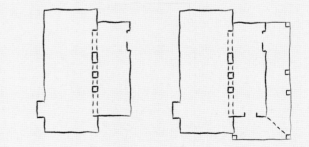

Although Tim and Susan are the new kids on the block, they didn't want their house to advertise the fact by looking like a suburban transplant. Architect Dale Mulfinger suggested designing what appeared to be "a house of accretion"—one that looked as though it had evolved over time. Classic farmsteads often began as modest gabled houses with additions built on as the

farm became established and the family grew. This gradual expansion was a highly visible symbol of a family's success, with the additions helping to establish the rootedness of the farm on the surrounding

land. The forms came together to create a large home that remains approachable in scale, yet graceful and proud.

A combined palette of painted and natural wood carries inside from the front porch. A clear finish is used on surfaces that get the most daily wear-and-tear—doors, cabinets, and benches. Other natural wood accents, like the mantel and ceiling beams, help tie the interior together.

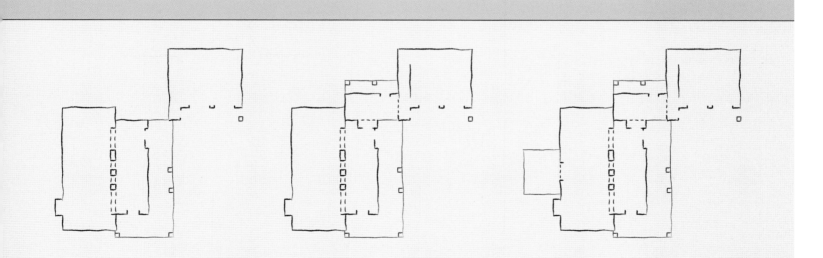

The bedrooms are tucked beneath the roof and, therefore, seem secure and comforting. Viewed from the outside, the lower roof line helps establish the proportions typical of many old farmhouses. The extended sill and apron trim detail at the windows gives an older feel to this new house.

French doors in the kitchen can freely be opened for a breeze because the screen porch is just beyond. A built-in bench, matching the bench in the adjacent living room, provides seating along one side of the table and leaves more room for circulation.

Three thresholds to the kitchen pass through a thickened wall, giving the sense of leaving the original stone home and entering an addition. Although the wood floor carries through both spaces, there is a shift from the beamed ceiling to one with painted V-groove boards. Openings to the kitchen and sunroom are graced with the same wood transom screen found at the entry bench. This screen is purely aesthetic, helping emphasize the separation between spaces without being opaque.

Early dinner guests never surprise Tim and Susan because the view from the kitchen sink extends past the prominent porch column to the entry lane. Looking in the other direction, the cooks can gaze through the dining area to the sunroom, with its views in three directions.

A side hall leads from the foyer to the support spaces of the house—a pantry, a half bath, and a

The kitchen is open to the main living area and yet clearly defined by a thickened wall, slatted transoms above each threshold, and a change from a beamed to a V-groove ceiling. The wall suggests the feeling of passing through an old exterior wall to an added room, and it also houses built-ins open to the kitchen.

The composition of the front facade sets up a strong sense of symmetry, then playfully breaks it. Where you might expect to see the front door, there is instead an over-size wood porch column. Although the column is carefully centered below the gable, the gable's asymmetry is emphasized by two small whimsical windows.

mudroom that connects to the attached garage. To direct visitors to the home's public rooms, the entrance to this service area is narrow and has a lower ceiling.

Upstairs, the secondary spaces are again organized in the center of the home, leaving the perimeter with access to light for the primary rooms. The master bedroom suite has windows on three sides for better air circulation and a feeling of spaciousness, even though it is tucked under the sloping roof.

Many visitors have paid Tim and Susan what the couple considers to be the highest of compliments, telling them they did a great job remodeling an old farmhouse. Although Tim modestly attributes the success of the design to Paul, any good house is in fact the result of owner, architect, and builder working in collaboration.

FIRST FLOOR

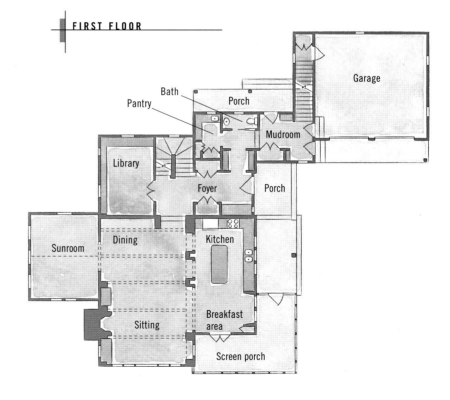

Blue Ridge Contrast

The main level of the farmhouse is several steps up from grade to keep the wood framing away from moisture and to provide daylight for the basement. In a clear departure from the norm, the new addition is set absolutely flush with the surrounding yard.

ELIZABETH AND ROBERT bought this farm some 30 years ago, enchanted by the wraparound views of the Blue Ridge Mountains and full of ideas for renovating the farmhouse. But their plans had to be put on hold: The farmer happened to come with the farm. He sold it on the condition that he be allowed to live in the old house and putter in the garden for the rest of his life.

Over the six years that followed, Elizabeth and Robert often visited the farm and eventually became good friends with their tenant, learning about the business of farming and the history of the house. By the time they moved in, their original plan to tear down walls and pop in French doors had evolved. The couple now felt committed to preserving the vintage farmhouse, along with the salt house, ice house, barns, and other accessory buildings that dated back to colonial times.

Nevertheless, they were determined to have a spacious room for entertaining—one that, unlike the existing living and dining rooms, would have windows that took advantage of the property's exceptional views.

The open doors of the glass pavilion reveal an inviting room, in contrast to the cool steel-and-glass exterior.

Expand and Contrast

A WELL-CONCEIVED ADDITION either blends seamlessly with the older house or stands in obvious contrast to it. Designs that fall somewhere in the middle run a high risk of looking like they are not quite here or there.

This farmhouse, built in 1799, is essentially a wood box with windows punched in the walls, and

the steel-framed living room pavilion of the new addition could hardly be more of a departure. The airy spaces with vaulted ceilings have an entirely different relationship to the outside than do the well-defined, contained rooms of the old house. Both stand as clear representations of the time in which they were designed and built. And both co-exist in a way that delights the owners.

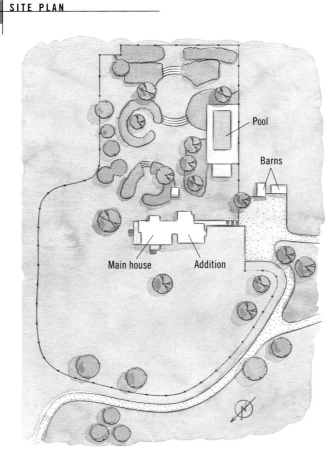

Pool

Barns

Main house   Addition

Contrasting Pavilions

The couple described their wishes to architect Robert Gurney, trying to avoid limiting his options with too specific a want list. As he studied the site from across the picturesque lawn, he envisioned a purely Modern design—a visually distinct form that would be respectful of the old house in a different way from which an addition blends in.

Robert presented his ideas, not knowing what sort of reaction he would get. The couple was silent at first—but with delight, not shock. They excitedly pulled out a favorite book on architect Philip Johnson's famous glass house, and the project was under way.

The addition takes the form of two pavilions sitting next to the farmhouse and seemingly separate from it. The larger pavilion, devoted to a living room, is a glass box with a black steel structure and a gable roof that appears to hover. The smaller pavilion, with a mudroom and bath, has a tall, steep gable and wood-clad walls with only a few windows. The two are a study in contrast: solid and void.

While clearly of this century, each pavilion has elements that relate back to the old house. The pitch of the larger pavilion's roof matches that of the farmhouse and the stone in its fireplace came from the land. In its footprint, the smaller pavilion is similar in size to the nearby salt house and its

At certain times of day, the all-glass facade reflects the landscape around it so that the black steel structure seems to frame a view of trees and countryside.

Pitched roofs, clapboard siding, and symmetry link these clean, Modern forms to the surrounding buildings. Set apart from its pavilion, the fireplace looks like the remnant of an earlier structure that the new room was built around.

The stone path is a transition zone between inside and outside. You don't really feel that you have entered the house until you step off the stone and onto the warm wood floor of the living room.

white clapboard matches the farmhouse's siding. The similarities, as you can see, stop there.

A Room with Glass Walls

The wide bluestone path to the house passes between the two pavilions and continues inside as flooring. This is one of a few ways in which the separation between outdoors and in has been all but erased, with a dramatic effect.

Elizabeth says that sitting in the living room of the larger pavilion is like being outside on a blanket in the grass, surrounded by the peaks of the Blue Ridge Mountains. The room is strikingly transparent, with walls of glass from floor to ceiling. In a departure from conventional practice, the lawn is at the same level as the finished floor, heightening the sense that there is no barrier

A Connected Cluster

An addition doesn't have to take the usual form of a bump-out or wing. The new spaces can be independent structures, or at least give that impression. In this project, each building has a distinct roof form that gives it a separate identity. The connections between the house and two pavilions are carefully designed to all but disappear.

A low, flat-roofed link between the house and glass pavilion is clad in copper and will develop a chocolate brown patina, making it recede as a dark shadow between old and new. On the other side of the house, a single large plate of glass creates a visual gap between the corner of the smaller pavilion and a corner of the farmhouse. With a little imagination, the cluster of buildings could be seen as a proud old farmhouse, a storage shed, and a high-tech corncrib, each with its own personality.

between indoors and out. Glass is all that divides the two. You almost find yourself relying on the Brazilian cherry wood floor and furniture for re-assurance that you are, in fact, inside.

In a similarly seamless way, the continuous wrapping band of transom glass dies into the underside edge of the white, vaulted ceiling. The roof, supported on its steel columns, seems to float overhead like a passing cloud. The columns are set back to further dematerialize the walls, allowing the large panes of glass to meet uninterrupted at the corner.

As visitors approach, the sharp-edged Modernism of the new addition gives little hint of the traditional white clapboard farm-house that lies just beyond.

The transparent walls bring the world outside into the interior, so much so that the furniture and maple built-ins almost look out of place. You expect to feel breezes blowing right through the room.

During the day, the white farmhouse stands out while the glass-walled pavilion looks almost black from a distance. The reverse occurs at night, when the pavilion is full of light and the house fades into the darkness.

FIRST FLOOR

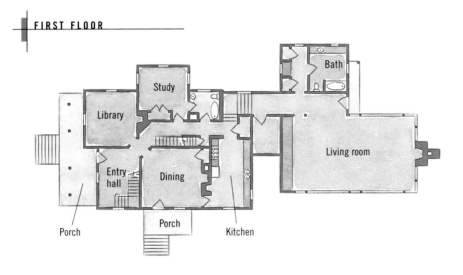

The stone-clad fireplace falls between two sets of tall steel-framed glass doors at one end of the room. The stone firebox extends outside the building, and its concrete flue is detached from the pavilion to avoid a break in the row of transom windows above the fireplace. The flue bears the linear markings and texture of the old barn wood used to form the concrete.

The smaller pavilion, just across the stone path, appears to be a solid box compared to the

The steel window frames of the living room provide the black outlines of a Mondrian painting, while the landscape adds the color. The room's strong symmetry gives it an air of both calm and formality.

In the smaller of the two pavilions, the stone floor, high ceilings, and doorlike window blur the lines between inside and out, even in the bathroom.

living room pavilion, but its few windows are carefully placed and have a drama of their own. A door-sized plate-glass window is aligned opposite the entry into both the mudroom and bathroom. Because it is frameless and extends down to the stone, the window looks like an open door that you might step right through to the outside.

At a glance, the original farmhouse looks entirely untouched by the project. But the corner at the end of the central path was redone with walls of glass, in a way that reconciles old and new sections of the home. The Modern aesthetic also flows into the renovated kitchen of the farmhouse, with its streamlined mahogany cabinets and rows of stainless-steel appliances. The room

Together, the roughness of the stone and the transparency of the plate glass give the sense that you are still outside as you head up the steps into the original structure. This corner marks the shift from old to new.

The tall white farmhouse remains the central focus of the site, as it has been for more than 200 years. The addition is less conspicuous, set back from a corner and lower than the old house.

has been reconfigured as a sleek workplace in which Elizabeth and Robert can comfortably cook up meals for a crowd.

The stark contrast of modern and historic forms serves both parts of the home very well. The owners find that the charm of the old is highlighted by the boldness of the new. Elizabeth and Robert get to enjoy both the familiar comforts of the old farmhouse and, just a few steps away, the startling beauty of a glass room.

The kitchen retains an original double-hung window with an interior shutter. In their simplicity, the modern lines of the renovation do not overwhelm the understated details of the old house.

A String of Barns

With its quiet color palette and collection of simple forms, this home sits as comfortably on the land as a traditional farmhouse.

A NEW FARMHOUSE WILL LOOK AS IF IT HAS ALWAYS BEEN there if the design draws on the forms of the local agricultural tradition. Marty and Michael hired architect Dail Dixon to help them create a modern homestead that would support their ideal of living more independently on the land. The couple chose a 30-acre parcel in the Piedmont of North Carolina, ideally located within two hours of the ocean in one direction and the Appalachian Mountains in the other. The land itself offered rolling hills, long views, and plenty of space for an orchard of heirloom fruit trees, a berry patch, a vegetable garden, and grazing pastures. Landscape architect Sam Reynolds was brought in to ensure that their new home would make the most of the site and the extensive gardens planned for it.

The design draws on the tobacco barns of the region, with their attached open-sided sheds. At first glimpse, the house appears to be a series of four separate "barns," as the architect and owners refer to them. But glass-walled links tie the home together, and an open-air pavilion extends to the three-car garage. By visually

Although the three barns that make up the home have the same width and roof pitch, they are distinguished by varying window patterns, hinting at the variety of spaces within.

Seen from inside the house, the pocket gardens are well-defined outdoor rooms that provide a textured foreground for the long pastoral views. Each garden has a distinct character, with plants chosen to thrive in their particular orientation to the sun.

Pasture woods

Pasture

Pond

Paddock

House

Barnyard

Maple woods

Pine woods

Berry patch

Orchard

Garden folly

N

The sense that the home is made up of independent structures is carried through to the interior. The view from side windows in the living room looks back on the adjacent link and barnlike structures.

breaking up the house in this way, Dail was able to avoid creating a formidably large structure that might overwhelm the site. The transparency of the glass-walled links also serves to bring in views of the adjacent gardens and make them part of Marty and Michael's interior.

Hard-Edged Yet Domestic

Taking the design a step further from a traditional house, there is no front door clearly centered in the front facade. This domestic symbol is set to one side, both to maintain the suggestion of a row of barns and to allow the landscape to remain the focal point.

Views, Long and Short

THIS HOUSE TAKES ADVANTAGE of both long views out over the landscape and intimate looks at the pocket gardens tucked alongside the walkway and just outside the windows.

One long linear view runs down the home's central corridor and continues out the main door, through the woods to the barnyard. This is the path Marty and Michael follow on their way to the orchard, garden, and berry patch. Another view intersects this one at the open entry pavilion, drawing visitors' attention to the patio overlooking the pond and pasture. A third, more subtle line of sight extends from the dining room windows to a cleared alley through the woods, ending at a circular glade that will someday have a sculpture as a focal point.

The walkway to the house passes through a cottage garden with a welcoming riot of pink and purple flowers. Outside the kitchen, the southern exposure suits the pocket herb garden and sun-loving plants such as black-eyed Susans. The gardens to each side of the dining room are planted with flowers that repeat the primary red and blue of the chairs; a gurgling fountain adds its music. A particularly shady pocket is planted in hydrangea and hosta varieties. There is a Southern tradition of planting highly fragrant plants just outside bedroom windows, and on summer evenings the master bedroom picks up scents from the adjacent flower garden.

From a distance, the gray walls of the barns look old, worn, and monochromatic, an impression reinforced by having relatively few windows on this side of the house. Only as visitors approach does a cheery palette of primary accent colors become apparent. There is a splash of red in the steel posts that support the pavilion roof, in the metal sun screens over south-facing windows, and in a starkly modern arbor. The exposed structure of the pavilion roof and the soffits of the house are painted a warm yellow, and the front door is bright blue.

The rooms that fall within the barns have 12-ft. ceilings and white oak floors, whereas those in the connecting links are distinguished

Like a plain coat with a colorful lining, the predominantly gray and glass house reveals its accent hues only as you are about to enter the front door.

A central circulation path extends the length of the house. Changes in flooring, wall cladding, and ceiling height all serve to highlight the segmented nature of the home.

by concrete floors, low sloped ceilings, and exterior walls of aluminum-framed store-front glazing. As a result, these links feel as though they were filled in years later, preserving the sense that the three barns are autonomous. There is an appealing rhythm to the various parts as you walk down the central corridor that runs the length of the house.

Another means of making the barns appear separate was to extend the exterior's vertical tongue-and-groove siding inside, as if the barns were joined over time. This is a way of building history into a house that has just been constructed. Even a plate-steel shelf can look like the vestige of an industrial relic rather than a new built-in.

A Different Take on the Farmhouse Kitchen

The kitchen, the first room inside the entry, is the home's center. Marty is a professionally trained cook, and her life revolves around the kitchen. Its location provides a convenient landing spot for fresh vegetables; a second door leads directly to the middle of the herb garden and a patio. High ceilings and lots of windows make this room feel spacious even during parties when everyone troops in to gather around the island. The island is nearly 12 ft. long and includes a sink-side cutout for compostable scraps.

The kitchen has a modern yet cordial aesthetic that is carried through the house. The tall white

The vertical tongue-and-groove siding is carried inside the glassy links, blurring the distinction between outdoors and in. Even the closet door looks like an exterior door to a utility shed.

This kitchen has endless counter space and enough open shelving for a serious cook. A stretch of windows provides views to help ensure that meal preparation will be an enjoyable process. The window sills are flush with the countertop, eliminating visual barriers between interior and exterior.

The sparely designed dining room doubles as a hallway between the living room and the kitchen. With a lower ceiling and walls of glass, this room draws the diner's eye out to the horizon.

walls have banks of windows below and small, square *punched* windows above, yielding more daylight than you'd find in a kitchen crowded with wall-mounted cabinets. The other half of this first barnlike unit is devoted to a guest room, bath, and playroom, placed here to provide privacy for the master bedroom at the far end.

The uncluttered dining room occupies one of the glazed links. It is furnished with only a table and a plate-steel buffet shelf hovering in front of the windows. The floor-to-ceiling *curtain walls* of glass allow the room to merge by day with the gardens to either side. In the evening, the glass walls become dark, and the focus turns inward to the food and conversation.

The second barn holds the principal living spaces. The living room is anchored by its ash cabinetry and fireplace, while windows wrap around three sides, taking in views to both the adjacent gardens and the open pasture. This public space is separated by a pair of doors from a library that is just the right size to accommodate two people. Its walls are paneled with cherry below and painted a dark blue hue above, giving the room an intimate feeling quite unlike the rest of the house.

The central corridor ends at a translucent glass block wall, glowing from behind with natural light. A turn at this wall leads into the

Windows Two Ways

In architecture, a single window surrounded by an expanse of wall is often called a *punched opening*. That sounds exotic, but punched windows are the typical sort of fenestration found in homes. They date back to colonial times, when glass was expensive and openings were kept small to save money and conserve heat.

A modern alternative is a *curtain wall*—a system of large glass panes set within a frame that takes the place of a traditional load-bearing wall. Since being introduced in commercial buildings, they have become affordable for domestic use, and double or triple panes with insulating gasses have made them more energy efficient. Still, most homes continue to stick with traditional punched openings. This house boldly plays the two types off one another, making for an interesting, invigorating mix.

The living room extends beyond the sides of the house for unobstructed views on three sides. Its south-facing windows are shielded by a metal sunshade.

A basic wood-burning fireplace unit was given a jacket of plate steel to transform it into a sleek, sculptural shadow box. One wing extends to keep wood storage out of view.

The foundation wall along the stair is clad in the ash panels used throughout the house, giving the lower level, with its two guest bedrooms, the same refinement as the main floor. The sandblasted glass block shares daylight and artificial light from the bathroom on the other side.

Although moderate in size, the master bedroom is served by a spacious bathroom and a pair of walk-in closets. The laundry room is just a few steps from the bedroom door.

last in the string of barns. The master bedroom is in one direction, and the laundry room is conveniently located in the other. The spaciousness of the 12-ft.-tall bedroom is grounded by the ash-paneled backdrop for the bed, while generously sized walk-in closets augment the room. Windows admit perfume from a fragrant garden of white-flowered plants just outside. A bathroom occupies the space behind the glass block wall; the same cherry wood used in the vanity base cabinet follows up the wall as a wood veneer behind the mirrors, giving the crisply white room a warm, tactile center.

The borrowed forms of the barns and sheds are overtly modern, with an industrial edge. Their rectilinear shapes are interwoven with the organic textures of the plantings and the landscape beyond. As innovative as this may sound, a traditional farmhouse and outbuildings do much the same: They introduce human-made elements to a bucolic setting, in ways we have come to think of as supremely picturesque.

The straightforward use of industrial materials carries into the bathroom, with its floors of concrete tile, precast concrete countertops, and sand-blasted glass block.

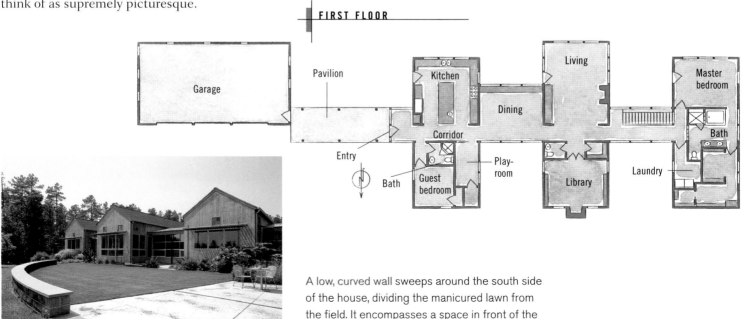

FIRST FLOOR

A low, curved wall sweeps around the south side of the house, dividing the manicured lawn from the field. It encompasses a space in front of the two more-public units of the home and does not reach the sanctum of the master bedroom.

This old farmhouse looks well nestled into its site. The two new wings of the house capture a courtyard that is given additional definition by a raised deck, a trellis, and an old tree.

A Farmhouse Takes Wing

WHEN THIS MODEST STORY-AND-A-HALF FARMHOUSE proved to be a magnet for their children and grandchildren, the owners decided to expand—cautiously. They realized that ambitious changes would threaten their home's endearing character. The house seemed to peek out through its dormer windows, and it was hardly a dominating presence on the farm's 130 acres of Minnesota fields and woods.

So the couple began the project with an ear tuned to the past, asking themselves how earlier owners of the farm might have gone about stretching the home. And they reassured the old house that it would be better off for all the changes.

"Don't mess it up," were their instructions to architect Tom Meyer. To that end, both the owners and the architect tried to avoid imposing too many firm requirements in the design; a six-burner industrial range or a three-car attached garage can lead down a path to a less-than-charming farmhouse that seems out of time and place.

The owners of this old farmstead have maintained the worn barn, silo, and windmill without stripping them of the endearing wrinkles that age brings.

The barn and the silo complement one another in function and form. Traditionally, they both played a part in housing and feeding livestock. The rectangular, horizontal shape of the barn sits firmly on the landscape, while the round vertical shape of the silo reaches up to the sky.

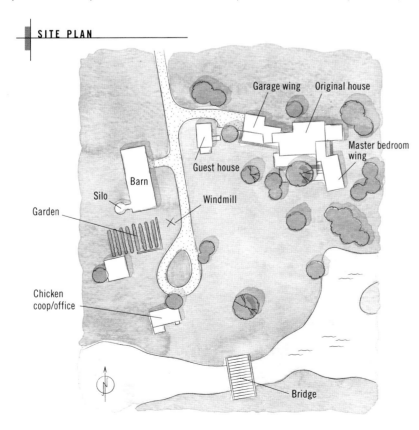

SITE PLAN

Garage wing   Original house

Master bedroom wing

Guest house

Barn

Silo   Windmill

Garden

Chicken coop/office

Bridge

True to the Core

Instead of grafting on one bulky wing that would handle all of his clients' needs, Tom designed three additions. He arranged them in such a way that the new pieces don't loom more important than the original structure. The old farmhouse remains the core, the hub of family life.

The approach to the house leads to a new wing, where porch steps spill down invitingly to greet visitors and family. The attached garage was kept to a single bay so that it wouldn't look intimidating.

Inside the relocated original door, there is no formal front foyer. One generous space serves all of the home's comings and goings. The bench that stretches along one wall is long enough for a clan of grandchildren to tie up tennis shoes or kick off snow boots. The stone floor in this room was laid by one of the homeowners' children, and

The new entry is kept informal by cladding both walls and ceiling with white-painted wood. A pass-through window to the kitchen provides a shortcut for groceries, a way to keep an eye on people arriving, and a spot for the grand-kids to set up an imaginary shop.

The inset porch serves as gateway to the house, and also as a loading and unloading zone and a place to just sit and watch the activities of the farm.

the pattern looks like a river winding its way into the farmhouse.

This wing is positioned at a slight angle to the house—11 degrees, to be exact. The quirky orientation is in the rural tradition of not neces-sarily troubling to align things exactly. Also, the canted addition seems less prominent because it trails away from the central form of the house.

At the far end of the house, the new master bedroom suite is also set at an 11-degree angle. The suite was planned as an independent part of the home, located just a few steps from the bustle of the gathered family. It is reached by passing through an unheated but enclosed link. This in-between space combines double-hung windows and a finished wood floor typical of an interior room. But there's a dramatic difference—the trellis-like ceiling is covered with a layer of translucent fiberglass for the effect of a light-filled

Porch rockers take in a view of the farm. The lights on the beefy columns are the no-nonsense sort of fixtures you might find illuminating the stalls of the barn.

Hanging in with Double-Hungs

OLD FARMHOUSES AND DOUBLE-HUNG WINDOWS are a perfect match. From the outside, they create a generous opening in the wall without losing a human scale; that's because the window is composed of two smaller halves, with both the upper and the lower sashes operable.

When renovating, replace these windows if need be, but think carefully before changing to another size or style. An old farmhouse with brand-new casement windows tends to look off-balance and uncomfortable with itself. Clear undivided panes of glass belong to houses of a different era. And because the large opening of a double-hung typically can't be filled with an operable casement window of the same size, two shorter windows may be needed to fill the space where there used to be one. The classic grace of the original proportions is lost.

Double-hung windows also suit a farmhouse because of their simple functionality. Traditionally, they operate on a system of weights and pulleys rather than

machine-made hardware; you can hear the satisfying *thunk* of the hidden sash weights talking back. These windows also do a good job of ventilating the house because they can be opened in different ways to promote air circulation. By inching open the upper sash, you let hot air out of the room, while the lower sash admits cooler air.

greenhouse. On the short trip to their quarters, the owners can enjoy the spatter of spring rains without getting wet. And in good weather, two exterior doors lure them to various parts of the yard. The owners find that this arrangement makes their hearts grow fonder both for the visitors in the house and (in cooler months) for the warming fire in the nearby living room.

A third wing is devoted to a dancing studio that doubles as a stage for performances by the grandchildren. This room has its own measure of separation, being reached by a hall that also connects to the master bedroom link. Together, the three wings add dramatically to the living area. But because the home is nestled in the property's old trees, you can never quite glimpse the entire house from any one vantage point.

The unheated link between the body of the house and the new master bedroom suite is an intriguing in-between space—neither inside, nor outside. With its flat roof and glass walls, the link attaches delicately to the old farmhouse.

The dining room is open to the living room and has a similar beamed ceiling. The traditional fixture over the table and the modern wall sconce and floor lamps all mix comfortably in this old house. As fits a farmhouse, the trim at the base, doors, and windows is simple yet substantial.

The link is a throwback to a kind of space that houses no longer tend to have—an enclosed un-heated area in which to store firewood or the leftovers from a holiday meal that don't fit in the refrigerator.

The second-floor bedrooms in this story-and-a-half farmhouse are tucked under the sloping rafters of the roof. They are kept light and airy with a palette of white for wall and ceiling boards as well as for trim. The dark wood furniture is crisply outlined against this background.

FIRST FLOOR

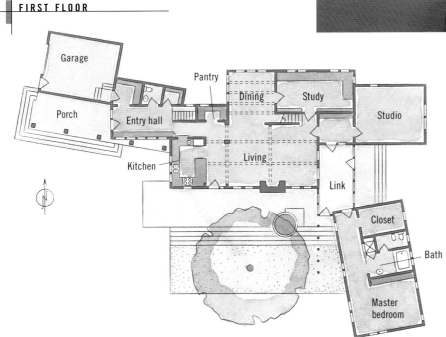

Garage

Porch

Entry hall

Kitchen

Pantry

Dining

Study

Studio

Living

Link

Closet

Bath

Master bedroom

Preserving the Best of the Rest

True to the owners' wishes, the renovation managed to preserve the integrity of the old farmhouse. Because the master bedroom suite is set apart, it doesn't share a wall with the home, and none of the living room's windows had to be sacrificed in the renovation. Connections between the living room, dining room, and kitchen were opened up, without losing the rooms' identities. Throughout the home, windows were restored rather than replaced, keeping the old glass with its way of casting watery light across the walls and floor. The living room retains its handsome coffered ceiling, and the beams remain intriguingly off center, as they have been for more than a century.

This sunny, unassuming kitchen foregoes upper cabinets and cabinet doors altogether. The open shelves are refreshingly practical, and the varied shapes and colors of the dishes decorate the room rather than relying on elaborate millwork.

Farmhouses are shaped by generations of past owners, including everything from new additions to marks on the trim noting the growth of the grandchildren. This is a style that grows old gracefully.

Another quirk discovered and embraced during the renovation is the fireplace. When it was stripped of its plaster cladding, the owners discovered the lower and upper halves had been built of different kinds of brick that likely were left over from masonry jobs. A new mantel was placed along the joint between the two to make a virtue out of the unusual combination. Overall, the changes in the existing house are significant but not dramatic—as when seeing a friend who has just gotten a fresh trim, it takes a while to figure out what is different.

The kitchen was redone, but that fact doesn't shout at you. Much of the storage is accomplished by open shelves—just boards on brackets, mounted on the biscuit-colored walls.

White House, Red Barn

A white house and a red barn—these are the classic symbols of the American farm. The house represents civilization, pressed and presentable. White is a color reserved for being clean, and that's a luxury on a farm, where dirt clods, manure, and hay seem to rule. Also, a white house stands out for miles against the blue sky and green fields, like a landlocked lighthouse.

The red barn, in contrast, is the place of animals and earthy, messy things—birth and death, sweat, and hard work. Barn red paint hides the dirt while complementing the surrounding green vegetation. From the approach drive, the red barn sits back, secondary to the white house. After centuries of this two-tone tradition, plastic and metal sidings have often replaced wood, but the white and red continue to delineate the worlds of human and beast.

When the two opposing sliding doors are open, the barn feels as if it were a bridge between the farmyard and the fields beyond. The view to the pasture is captured like a frame in a slide show.

The home's added rooms have changed the way the family lives, of course, yet the owners say that the key to their farmhouse's revival isn't just the new spaces. They give credit to something that might be overlooked on a stroll through the renovated rooms: the cocked angle at which the garage and master bedroom additions were spliced onto the original structure, which has changed the property's personality. It's as if the old house were reaching out its arms to the surrounding farm, like a grandmother embracing a younger generation.

Farm outbuildings are charming and recognizable because their forms follow from their function. The circular fins of the windmill reach up to catch the breeze, and the barn has doors sized for both people and tractors.

This traditional farm-house occupies a traditional site—atop a rise in the landscape, nestled into a protective grove of trees. Even with its weathered siding, it stands out on the horizon as the deep-colored barn recedes like a shadow.

Barn with a Past and Future

As Ann crested a hill just outside Weston, Missouri, she caught her first glimpse of the abandoned farmhouse that would be her home. The metal hipped roof was falling down, allowing trees to grow from within. Her first impulse might have been to bulldoze the house and start over. Instead, she dug in and brought the place back to life over the next three years.

The house had been a weathered gray, with only traces of the old white paint left on the horizontal clapboard siding. To maintain this time-softened look, Ann chose to have the new clapboard stained, rather than painting it the gleaming white typical of farm-houses in the region. For Ann, the farmhouse represented her past—the history and memories that inform the values that make her who she is today. She also felt that the property wasn't complete without a barn. The barn would not only be a place to park the car and tractor but would also provide a free-form, open-ended space to spark creativity.

The barn is simultaneously raw and refined. The design is sophisticated, and yet the structure is unheated and without screens—open to breezes, bugs, and birds.

The canopies that shade the large openings look as though the copper siding were cut, folded up out of the way, and then propped open on metal struts. This detail brings to mind the casual character of a corrugated cardboard box that has been made into a playhouse, with openings cut to make windows and doors.

From the house, trees help camouflage the large size of the barn. A wide entry ramp wraps down to create a smooth transition into the barn, where the owner holds everything from quiet dinners to design seminars.

BARN: FIRST FLOOR

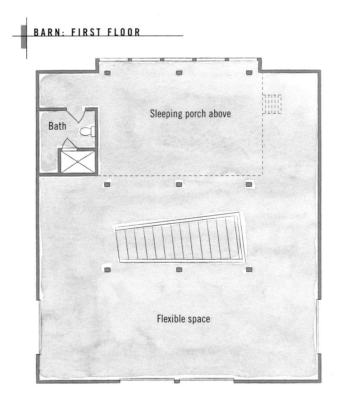

Bath

Sleeping porch above

Flexible space

Barnstorming for a Barn

Ann and architect Dan Maginn began by meeting with a local company that builds pole barns, designed practically and economically to meet the needs of working farmers. But the structures lacked the creative spirit that Ann was after. Driving back from the meeting, Ann and Dan pulled into a demonstration farm for school groups. Serendipitously, the farm owners happened to have for sale the frame of a barn that was due to be disassembled and moved. They also had a scale model of that frame, which helped stir Ann's imagination. She and Dan talked over the possibility of moving the old frame from northern Kansas to her site, and soon she was writing a check.

Traveling to Kansas, they found that the barn was a sublime ruin, with sunlight spilling through the gaping roof onto the timbers—a sight that was to inspire them in designing the barn as a light-filled, open structure. The pieces of the frame were numbered, dismantled, and stored in a grain silo to await delivery to their destination in Missouri. Ann agreed with Dan that the barn should be "straightforward yet spirited," as she put it. They felt that if their design derived from the barn's original use, the result would feel authentic rather than resembling a kitsch reproduction.

The barn was intended to serve a variety of functions. Its open, flexible space was suited to carving out a painting studio as well as a setting for social and business gatherings. On a practical level, Ann needed to shelter a car, a tractor, and assorted implements. There would be a private bedroom niche in the sleeping loft as well.

Old Begets New

AN INNOVATIVE DESIGN that is grounded in the past will bear the test of time. In this project, the old barn frame is a foothold in the familiar, while unusual materials and details stretch the design into the future. The recycled bones of the original structure set the scale and proportions for the new building. Although the copper and fiberglass cladding, the sliding glass barn doors, and the industrial awnings push well beyond tradition, the building is still unmistakably a barn.

When renovating an old farmhouse, consider preserving some of the endearingly crusty, well-worn parts. All five senses affect our experience of a house. The scraped paint on the front door combines with the slam of the screen door to express the spirit of this place.

Ann was concerned that the barn might overwhelm the modestly scaled farmhouse, and care was taken to have it set back into the side of a hill. From a distance, only the upper half of the structure can be seen at first, so that its size isn't immediately apparent. Also, the barn has receded somewhat from view over time because its copper cladding, once bright and shiny, has taken on the flat color of an old penny so that it blends in with the surrounding vegetation.

The proportions of this barn are familiar and traditional because they were determined by the reused timber frame. However, the copper siding has an unfamiliar, abstractly modern aesthetic. As with a classic old barn, the simple facade disguises the structural drama to be found inside.

With the large glass barn doors and a flood of daylight from the translucent roof, the barn has a warm glow even on cloudy days.

In the back bay of the barn, the translucent fiberglass provides an abstract view of nature with the shadow silhouettes of the trees outside. As in many barns, there is a ladder to the loft, but this upper level is used for sleeping, not storing hay.

Copper siding gives way to translucent fiberglass, exposing the structure of the barn in the intriguing way that cut-away models reveal the interior workings of machines.

A See-Through Skin

The barn's overall form is conventional, but its skin is wrapped in opaque corrugated copper in some places and translucent fiberglass panels in others. The effect is dramatic inside and out.

One gable end has a cantilevered row of windows, some operable, set within a translucent fiberglass wall that wraps around to the adjacent sides of the barn. The barn's skeleton is visible from the outside, exposing the structure like the unsheathed balsa wood model frame that originally caught Ann's attention.

The walls are also punctured with huge openings the size of barn doors that bring in views of the farm, and much of the roof is fiberglass panels that illuminate the reconstructed timber frame. The large windows can be slid open, and metal railings allow people to lean out to enjoy fresh air and the landscape.

In the rural tradition of designing buildings as they are built, an additional narrow roof panel of fiberglass was spontaneously added, washing the back wall of the barn with warm light. Natural and artificial light is allowed to pass from level to level by stopping the floors short of the barn walls. This unusual feature gives a floating sense to the spaces built within the barn.

Because much of the barn remains open, first-time visitors are awestruck by the overarching network of old beams. The barn's three framed sections, or *bays,* visually divide the structure. A stairway in the center bay connects the garage on the lower level with the main space. In a back corner of the barn, a freestanding utility tower rises up through the structure; it contains a mechanical room at the ground floor, a bathroom

This bathroom seems to be a series of flat planes brought together to contain a space. Slightly darker tile wraps up the wall and around the room to playfully mimic a waterline just below knee level.

Modern wood-clad walls were inserted within the forest of the timber frame to delineate the stair from below, a window seat under the loft, and the bathroom. These clean, flat surfaces contrast with the exposed frame and highly textured siding of the exterior walls.

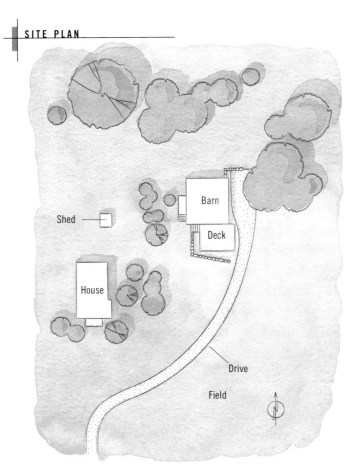

above that, and a private sleeping nook up at the level of a hayloft.

The flexible floor plan allows Ann to invite groups of any size. She might have dinner for two, set a table for 10 and wheel in a grand piano, or organize a design seminar for 50. The uninsulated roof and exposed frame highlight the contrasting materials, combining old hand-planed timbers with the copper cladding.

Ann also points out that there is a marked contrast between the personalities of the barn and the house. With its small scale, pastel walls, and white trim, the house strikes her as feminine, and it is anchored reassuringly in the past. The barn, on the other hand, is a spare and rugged setting in which creative people gather

FARMHOUSE STYLE

Humble Is Hip

The design of an older home can tell you a lot about the availability of building materials at the time it was built. Milled lumber is a case in point. As the railroads made their way across the country, pre-cut studs and rafters became an affordable alternative to large timber beams. These lengths placed some constraint on the shape and proportions of houses.

This old farmhouse is an example. Its narrow proportions minimized the need for long timbers. The hipped roof allowed using an economical mix of

long and short rafters. The spare use of windows suggests that the house had humble beginnings, as does the mishmash of scrap building materials discovered when the house was renovated.

The house may owe its survival to the quiet charm of its straightforward form and materials—a quality often lacking in new, needlessly large houses. Today, humble is hip.

to think outside the box. Both structures can be experienced at the same time and each is more interesting because of its pairing with the other. While sipping lemonade on the porch of the farmhouse, Ann and her visitors can watch as evening turns the barn into an oversized lantern, glowing from within.

Time is kind to honest materials. Both the farmhouse's horizontal clapboard and the barn's darkening copper siding are improved by the patina of age and the elements.

Floor-to-ceiling screens are an almost invisible barrier between inside and outside. The view from the porch encompasses the past, symbolized by the stone foundation walls of former corncribs, and also the innovative, futuristic barn that peeks out from behind the trees.

A Farm Full of Projects

Early farmers typically planted a grove of trees to protect the house from the prevailing winds in the winter and to provide a cooling shade in the summer. From a distance, a cluster of trees adjacent to a wide open field is the first visual clue of the farmhouse sheltered within.

A BEAUTIFUL NEWEL POST was the bait that drew Jennifer and Robert to look at a large old house in New Jersey. Robert spotted a mention of the ornate detail in an Internet real estate listing, and that was enough to spur visions of trading in their small Cape Cod in the city for a big old Victorian farmhouse.

On their first visit, they discovered that the newel post was in fact the highlight of the entire property. The house and its porches were in disrepair. And although the place was still owned by the third generation of the original family, its finishes and cladding were anything but original—everything inside was painted green, and the outside was wrapped in white aluminum siding.

This would be a remodeling project that had more to do with peeling away layers than adding on space. Nevertheless, Jennifer and Robert could see the potential beneath the rough spots, and the beautiful setting also helped make the sale. The 5-acre property is adjacent to 150 acres of deed-restricted agricultural land, so the open fields will not fall prey to a suburban subdivision.

With their bay windows, turrets, and overall asymmetry, Victorian farmhouses broke out of the traditional Colonial box. This house has the cross-gabled form, scalloped siding, lace-like brackets, and elaborate chimney brickwork typical of the Victorian substyle known as Queen Anne.

Victorian houses often had more than one porch, and this farmhouse has them on the front, side, and back. Over the course of a day, the family can follow the sun—or avoid it, depending on the season.

Unwrapping a Victorian

Jennifer and Robert were well aware of the need to pull up shag carpet, peel off aluminum siding, shore up sagging bays, and replace old windows. But they were less certain about how to approach the bigger issues—designing a new kitchen and master bedroom and reworking two sore-thumb additions. They asked architect Rich Carroll for help.

As the aluminum siding came off, the couple was pleasantly surprised to find that the original clapboard siding was in good shape. The restoration included scraping and painting the scalloped siding on the upper bays and gable ends as well as the ornamental *darts* just below the fascia— elements that add the texture characteristic of the style. Although the window trim had been cut to attach the aluminum, enough of the original Victorian profile remained to serve as templates for making new trim.

The exterior detail operates on two levels. It adds texture and shadow from a distance, but on a closer scale it is possible to appreciate the intricacies of the brackets and trim.

Victorian Farmhouses

The Victorian era coincided with the mass production of lumber and inexpensive bric-a-brac. Traditional timber-frame construction was replaced by lightweight balloon frames of 2x4 lumber. These frames could be easily erected by less-experienced carpenters, and their flexible placement made it possible to create the bay windows, turrets, and dormers typical of the Victorian style.

Compared to the earlier Colonial style, Victorian houses have complex, asymmetrical plans and are clad with elaborate textures. Pastel colors and exuberant detail are both indicative of the optimism of the time. Because of a popular obsession with fresh air, these houses had plentiful porches—front, back, up and down, and even sleeping porches. Victorian farmhouses tended to be practical, pared-down variations

on the style. You'll often see straightforward gabled forms, dressed up with brackets under the eaves, and porches that incorporate turned spindles and jigsaw trim.

While much of the original interior was reworked to open the floor plan, the newel post, railing, and double front doors were left intact. The piece of art glass above the front door looks original, but it was salvaged from another building. While most of the house is in the Queen Anne style, the double entry doors (and the round-top windows in the gables) could be called Italianate.

In the living room, an efficient woodstove provides the heat instead of a drafty fireplace. However, there is a decorative fireplace surround in keeping with the style of the period. The surround is of stone, painted with a marble faux finish.

Victorian rooms typically were isolated from one another, in a way that doesn't feel comfortable for today's families. Inside this home, the main-floor living spaces had already been opened up in an earlier remodeling, with a series of graceful arched openings marking the transitions. While the rooms retain their traditional definition, the sweeping arches provide views from front to back in a way that unifies the house.

The 10-ft.-high ceilings allow use of elegantly tall double-hung windows. New wood units were custom made with the original muntin patterns, preserving the graceful proportions of the old windows. The plaster ceiling in the family room still has a medallion decorated with fruit, suggesting that this was originally the dining room.

Working through a Maze

While the main living spaces didn't need much more than their surfaces refinished and windows replaced, the back half of the house was dramatically rearranged. Rich called for walls to be taken out and openings reworked. The kitchen and mudroom, added some years before, had a limited connection to the rest of the house, and

The clutter and noise of the kitchen is kept at bay with a tall furniture-like piece of cabinetry. The division between kitchen and dining room is also marked by the framed section of art glass hanging from the ceiling.

As is often the case in older kitchens, the tall double-hung windows were replaced with shorter units to allow running a continuous countertop along the exterior walls. The L-shaped island includes a spot for a breakfast bar, out of the main working area of the kitchen.

The new double-hung windows with a single vertical muntin and the trim with wood corner blocks match the details elsewhere in the house.

the new arrangement does away with the old maze of doors and walls. The new kitchen is connected to the dining room on one side and the new breakfast room on the other. Although it's located where the old kitchen had been, the open design makes the new room feel twice as big while also allowing more countertops and cabinets.

The center island is equipped with a vegetable sink, and it provides a place to pull up a stool for a light meal. The island is backed up by a three-quarter-height cabinet wall that elegantly separates the formal dining room from the kitchen and provides display shelves and handy storage for table linens. The threshold between the two rooms is also defined by an antique stained glass window that hangs from above. The breakfast room is brightened by banks of tall double-hung windows on two sides. It is used throughout the day, with a desk nook for the computer and paperwork.

Interior trim became highly ornate during the Victorian era. Wood corner blocks were used at windows and doors to add an extra flourish, while also simplifying the joint between the complex profiles of vertical and horizontal millwork.

The tall second-floor bathroom window was kept as is to preserve the regular rhythm of the exterior composition. Shelves step out to subtly divide the room into two halves, providing an alcove for the toilet.

Bay windows, a traditional means of flooding a room with daylight, may have a window seat or be left open for more floor space. When the windows reach the floor, the extension can make you feel as though you are in the treetops.

As on the floor below, the plan of the original front half of the house remains much the same on the second level. Two window bays create inviting light-filled niches that animate each of the front bedrooms. But the layout at the back, involving an old addition, was muddled. Closets were inefficiently placed, and two stairs ran up to the attic. Additions like this can be reworked to seamlessly connect with the original house. After a tour of the house with the homeowners, the architect begins the design by placing tracing paper (known in the trade as "bumwad") on the existing floor plan, then rearranging the pieces of the puzzle until a solution is found. In this house, walls were moved to convert four bed-rooms and one bath into three bedrooms, a bath, and a master suite. A small gabled addition helps resolve the awkwardness of the earlier flat-roofed addition.

Buying a gangling old farmhouse takes vision and daring because you can never be quite sure what you'll find until you begin remodeling. For Jennifer and Robert, however, this home had a soul that was worth preserving, and its long history has added to their satisfaction of ownership. The couple knows of weddings celebrated on the farm, the mailman recalls playing there as a child, and people spontaneously show up on the porch to share their memories of the house.

Small Addition, Big Transformation

WHEN THE INTERIOR of a farmhouse is reworked, space can be used more efficiently, the circulation between rooms flows better, and long views through the house make it seem larger. The bottom line? The remodeled house may need only a small addition—one that costs less and fits in discreetly.

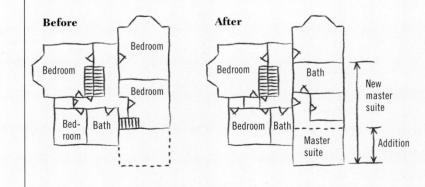

The original siding, bracket design, and window trim were carried through to earlier additions, making it hard to tell where old stops and new starts. The unpaved driveway with its casual curve is in keeping with the home's setting.

Pavilions
in the Pasture

AFTER RAISING A FAMILY IN LOS ANGELES, Janice and Joel found themselves empty nesters and ready for a change of scene. Joel was now able to telecommute, freeing the couple from having to live in a particular place, and they searched northern California with the intention of buying a rural home. Most of the properties they saw seemed less like farmhouses than suburban transplants, so they began looking instead for land and an architect.

Janice and Joel found a 6-acre parcel of old cow pasture in Sonoma County and fell in love with the open green fields. They approached architect Patricia Motzkin with a folder full of magazine clippings and several design goals: fresh air and natural light; a Craftsman sense of material and detail; a hardworking, up-to-date kitchen; and a house that would be functional, beautiful, simple, and classic.

With its several gables, the house looks something like the clustered outbuildings of a farm. On a broad, open site, this approach helps settle the home in the landscape.

157

Concrete Isn't Just for Basements

MOST OF US THINK OF CONCRETE as a cold, hard material for basements, garages, and sidewalks. But this flexible, practical option is virtually indestructible, and textures and patterns can be added for visual interest. Also, color can be either applied or stirred right in as the material is mixed. Concrete will expand and contract, so expansion joints are a must; however, this practical necessity can become a well-integrated part of the design, as with the handsome red floor of this house. The dimensions of its grid are carefully coordinated with those of the millwork and the placement of doors.

Low and Linear

As the couple and their architect took walks on the site, the design began to take shape. The main living spaces occupy the middle section of the house, which offers the best and broadest views. Four pavilion-like rooms anchor each corner of the house. These contain the more private areas, including guest bedrooms, master bathroom, and a home office. The house is primarily on one level, with a couple of advantages—there are many opportunities to connect to the outdoors, and Janice and Joel will find it easy to grow old here.

The design is inspired by nearby agricultural buildings. The red siding and white trim are a natural fit with the home's simple gabled forms,

Throughout the house, details have a straightforward simplicity inspired by agricultural buildings in the area. The matte tiles of the fireplace share this practical, utilitarian spirit.

The long, low house settles comfortably into the landscape. From the road, the view extends right over the rooftops to the fields beyond.

The simple gables, clad in red board-and-batten siding and trimmed with white, feel right at home in this former cow pasture. While the rooflines of the two bedroom pavilions mirror each other, one is set lower and its taller window adds an interesting twist to this minimal facade.

which themselves are suited to this rural setting. The walls contrast vividly with the green vegetation during wet times of the year and complement the golden hues in the dry months.

The office pavilion stretches upward to recall the water towers once typical of the region, and the exterior board-and-batten siding is commonly associated with farm structures. The house has been laid out along the hill in way that is unassuming; it takes advantage of the view without dominating the landscape. From the road, the pavilions at the ends are not prominent and the house looks like another layer in the landscape, with the horizon line beyond. A series of dock-like terraces steps down through a blanket of green vegetation to the long, low house.

From the front vestibule, a strategically placed maple display niche provides a focal point for the entry while limiting views of muddy boots and wet umbrellas from the living spaces. The grid on the concrete is coordinated with the threshold and niche.

You can't judge a book by its cover: Within this modest-looking house are quietly impressive modern spaces. The divider between living and dining rooms stops short of the ceiling to emphasize the continuous vault.

Following the Grain

The exterior of the house is understated; step inside, however, and you can see the sophisticated influence of the owners' urban sensibilities. From the entry vestibule, visitors are presented with a carefully composed display niche that hints at the character of the rooms beyond. The house manages to look both cleanly practical and graciously welcoming.

The interior walls are clad with simple maple paneling, creating a warm yet modern room. Wall sconces throw light on the ceiling for an ambient source of illumination that supplements the direct lighting. A freestanding fireplace is set within a maple-clad partition that defines the dining room. Similarly, a television cabinet separates the living room from the hall to the bedrooms.

A subtle angle in the floor plan creates a wedge of space between the dining room and kitchen—just enough area to squeeze in a pantry.

FARMHOUSE STYLE

A Dash of Regional Flavor

When early American farmers migrated to the West Coast they found a climate well suited for agriculture but in need of irrigation. The water towers and irrigation systems of California's Central Valley turned this region into one of the world's most important agricultural centers.

The distinctively squat proportions of these towers evolved out of practical need. They were typically framed with wood and had a pump room at the base. An upper cantilevered portion holds the tank, giving the tower its distinctive form. Quirky regional features like these can be referenced to bring a new farmhouse out of the ordinary while helping place it in a vernacular tradition.

A two-sided, freestanding fireplace separates the living room from the dining room, and the straight-forward maple paneling echoes the sensibility of the board-and-batten exterior siding.

The lowered ceiling above the window seat makes it feel like a place of refuge within the larger vaulted space of the bedroom. Both recessed lighting and the adjacent window make this the perfect spot to catch up on the latest book stacked on the night stand.

The kitchen has elbow room, and the vaulted ceiling and floating upper cabinets make it feel even more spacious (see the photo on p. 165). A large center island provides enough countertop area for chopping vegetables and hanging out with family and friends. The blond wood and spare lines are consistent with the rest of the house.

Beyond the kitchen, the master bedroom is connected to the master bath pavilion and office tower. Set three steps down from the bedroom, the office is in a removed corner that makes it a spot for working free from household interrup-

tions. The high tower windows can be opened to
let the breezes blow without disturbing paperwork on the desks below. On the opposite end of
the house, each guest room is set in its own
pavilion with a bath tucked between.

A Simple Palette

Although the house appears from a distance to
be a scattering of outbuildings, the main living
spaces flow together coherently in part because
of the restrained choice of materials. The floor
throughout the house is of concrete, patterned
with a 4-ft. grid and colored a rich red hue. This
humble raw material appears refined as it is used
here, and in the evening the maple panels pick
up an amber glow from the floor.

At just 16 ft. across, the narrow floor plan lets
natural light fill the main living spaces from
morning to afternoon. French doors open up to a
patio, which is set three steps down from the
house so that its chairs and table don't interrupt
the view from inside. And because it's only three
steps up from the ground, no railing is required.
When the field grasses are high, the experience
of sitting on the patio feels like being on deck in
a sea of green. A simple wood trellis shades the
patio and house from the hot western sun, and
vegetation has been planted next to the house to
provide a break from the ocean winds that blow
constantly in the afternoon.

The vertical proportions of the office are highlighted by the tall windows, and yet the height
of the space is kept in check with a change of
paint color above and below a continuous
band of trim near the ceiling.

The patio extends out from the living room and dining room, taking advantage of the site's best long views. This outdoor space feels like a room itself, with the same red concrete floor used inside, a wood trellis overhead, and pavilions that protrude at each end to suggest side walls.

FIRST FLOOR

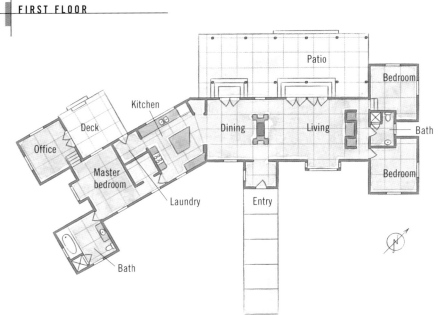

Good design attempts to anticipate how a building will work, but it may yield pleasant surprises as well. To accommodate the contours of the site, Patricia built a "kink" or elbow into the design. Once the house was constructed, Janice and Joel were pleased to find that views from the large windows of the living area include the ends of the house—much as you might glimpse the engine or caboose from the dining car of a train as it rounds a bend. This unusual perspective visually connects all the pieces of the design. And it is emblematic of the way in which two urbanites have successfully planted roots in a rural landscape.

In following the contour of the land, the house makes a slight bend, as reflected in the grid on the concrete floors and in the triangular shape of the kitchen island. Maple cabinetry maintains a simple, unified palette with the adjacent living spaces.

The back facade, like the other sides of the house, is calmly ordered in its symmetry.

Farmhouse as Fun House

SITUATED AT A CROSSROADS IN THE CORNFIELDS, this eye-catching metal house with its colorful roof is sure to become a local landmark. The home stands at the intersection of the familiar and the innovative, the domestic and the industrial, in ways that stretch the notion of a farmhouse without losing a sense of its heritage.

It's possible to be drawn to an old farm and yet want to give its conventions a tweak. This farmhouse, located just a few miles from the dunes along the eastern shore of Lake Michigan, was a classic one-and-a-half-story rural house with worn wood siding and a symmetrical layout. Paul and Bettylu changed that, working with architect Margaret McCurry, an old friend. The result is a farmhouse that looks fairly traditional from a distance but reveals an attitude as you approach.

From a distance, the dark window frames and checkered roof are hints that this farmhouse has been given a new lease on life through a renovation. The row of three small gables in the center section makes the home look as though it were stretched like an accordion.

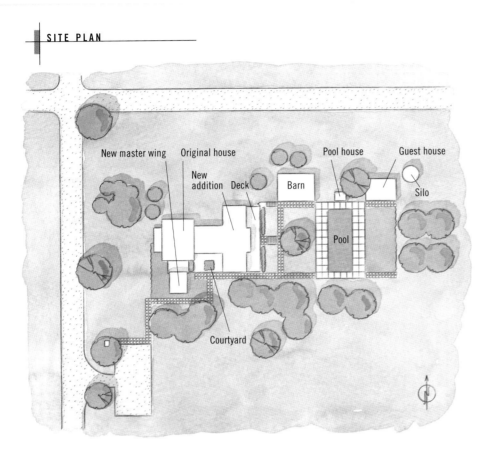

New master wing   Original house

New
addition   Deck

Barn

Pool house

Guest house

Silo

Pool

Courtyard

Both Practical and Playful

Paul and Bettylu asked that the remodeled house be able to hold their four adult children and eight grandchildren—all on the same weekend. Margaret's solution was to embed the old farmhouse within a new, larger structure. The design takes its inspiration from the original symmetrical form, one and a half stories high and topped by a gable roof. But the organization of the house was dramatically changed, along with the siding.

Gone is the comfortably familiar white clapboard common to Midwestern farmhouses. Margaret chose corrugated metal siding for an inexpensive, maintenance-free exterior. On the original portion of the house, this siding runs horizontally in the manner of clapboard, while the new addition is distinguished by its vertical pattern. This simple device makes it possible to identify the older structure, while preserving the coherence of the overall design.

Viewed from a distance, the collection of well-kept buildings retains the look of a traditional farm. In the thick of summer when the pool is in daily use, the corn is tall enough to form a living privacy wall.

Even a birch tree conforms to the geometric balance of the house, centered in the terrace and aligning with the chimney beyond. The garden shrubs are also placed with care, as if they were architectural elements.

If considered creatively, and even playfully, obsolete outbuildings can have second lives as guest quarters, studios, and playhouses. This old outhouse has been relocated close to the road and now serves as a garbage shed.

Guests in this farmhouse might find that going upstairs to bed is quite an event, involving an ascent up a spiral stair, then walking along the gangway of the bridge to the extra bedroom tucked under the eaves.

The style of the new windows also makes a connection between old and new. Although the windows are classic double-hungs and spaced conventionally (rather than being ganged together to make a wall of glass), there are no traditional muntins dividing the glass into smaller panes. The playful checkered roof was influenced by the regional practice of making patterns and even spelling out initials and names on the

IN DETAIL

Roof Play

FARMHOUSES TRADITIONALLY have been constructed of humble, economical materials, and the asphalt shingles of this checkerboard roof are a conventional choice applied in an unconventional pattern. The simple gable forms of the classic Midwestern farmhouse look good with a colorful hat. Other variations on the familiar include applying contrasting colors in stripes, and doubling up courses every 10th course or so to add subtle texture to the flat roof plane.

This airy vaulted space is a clear departure from the boxy rooms of a traditional farmhouse. This home stays at a safe distance from nostalgia through its use of steel and concrete.

shingled roofs of barns. Even the roof form itself is energetic, with a series of small gabled peaks.

Like many older farmhouses, this one had a seldom-used formal front door facing the road—most people by-passed it to enter the side door to the kitchen at the true center of the home. In the new design, the front door is gone, and visitors now approach the side of the house across a patio held between two new wings on the way to the main entry. The metal siding prepares them for what comes next—a bridge of black steel I-beams that soars across the vaulted kitchen and dining room.

This structure is yet another aspect of the home that is at once practical and playful. Grandchildren can display art projects and launch paper airplanes from the bridge. The bridge also serves as a second-floor link between the original farmhouse, with its dormlike bedrooms, and the new guest room.

Boarding-House Reach

In harmony with the bridge, the kitchen cabinets and island are of no-nonsense stainless steel. Even the chairs pulled up to the long dining table are of durable metal. A stainless-steel mechanical line runs unapologetically along the ridge in plain view. As elsewhere, the new floors are made of hardworking concrete.

Just as the stretched-out dining table looks like something out of a boarding house, the upstairs

Although the gable forms are familiar, the front door remains elusive. The architect has composed the entry in a starkly Modern fashion.

of the original house wing now *feels* like one, with a pair of second-floor sleeping lofts each having a row of four beds for the grandchildren. To accommodate visiting adults, there are two more bedrooms on the floor below. These lower bedrooms share their own screen porch, which replaces the original front stoop. With all of that company under the roof, the owners can retreat to a master bedroom suite that extends out from the house, buffered from noises within the home by an entry hall that is lined with closets.

This farmhouse was planned with children in mind, and there are whimsical details built into the design. A door from one sleeping loft opens onto a sequestered second-floor deck, which in turn leads through another door back inside to a "kids-only" hideout, tucked in the attic space above the master bedroom.

Once the most public part of the house, the former front facade now has a private screen porch shared by the two adjacent bedrooms. The white grid of its framing forms an abstract design, much as the shingles do up on the roof.

Rural Renewal

Heading the other way through the kitchen and dining area, you come to the living room, flanked by a screen porch and sunroom. Although there is no wall separating the living room from the activities of cooking and dining, it is defined and made more intimate by its flat ceiling. In line with the home's industrial aesthetic, the living room's fireplace is of unadorned concrete blocks. The ceiling soars again as you enter the sunroom to one side or the porch to the other. These rooms mirror each other in size and shape, and both connect to the yard with doors in three directions. The light flooding into them is shared with a second-floor guest bedroom through interior windows.

It adds to Paul and Bettylu's appreciation of the farm that their fields are still being worked.

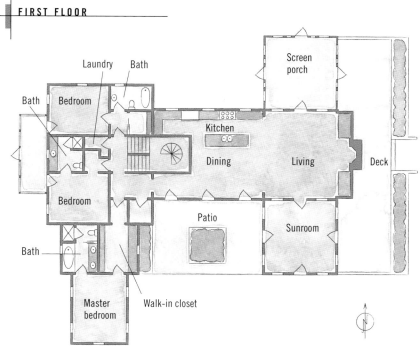

FIRST FLOOR

Laundry Bath
Bath Bedroom
Kitchen
Bedroom
Dining Living Deck
Master bedroom Walk-in closet
Bath
Bedroom
Patio Sunroom
Screen porch

The central space of the house receives an extra quota of daylight through the high, square window in each of the small gable dormers. The wood dining table stands out as a warm highlight in the space dominated by steel; and in a tall room that might otherwise be intimidating, the bridge helps establish a comfortably human scale.

Concrete block is usually relegated to foundations. Here it is featured as the focal point of the living room, making no attempt to dress up the humble material with stucco or even a coat of paint.

of them as possible, partly out of respect for the local descendants of the farmer who had built the house by hand. Margaret reconfigured the property by taking out those outbuildings that were in the way and relocating others. Like dead-heading a bouquet of flowers, this reorganization brought a new life to the farm. The line of structures now serves to screen the farm from the occasional passing car or tractor, and it also frames one side of the pool terrace.

The milking shed, with its arched Quonset hut roof, intrigued both architect and home-owners, and it was moved and made into a pool house. The barn still houses a tractor, which is primarily used to give the grandchildren hayrides. The old pig barn was cleaned up to become a pool-side guesthouse, and its original pig-size openings have been glazed in as a reminder of the former inhabitants. The silo is soon to be converted into a playhouse for the kids. Even the outhouse has a new job. It marks a turn in the driveway and allows garbage cans to be stored out of the reach of hungry raccoons.

They get to enjoy the fruits of their own land without giving up their day jobs. The previous owner continues to rotate corn, soybeans, pumpkins, and squash. In addition, the Concord grapes grown here are used in making Welch's jelly.

Paul and Bettylu also value the farm's scattering of outbuildings. They wanted to retain as many

FARMHOUSE STYLE

Designing with Restraint

The character and charm of old farmhouses and outbuildings are in part the result of constraints. At the time these structures were built, materials were few and locally produced; the available technology had been handed down for generations. Whether dealing with post-and-beam construction or dimensioned lumber, builders worked with the technology and materials available.

Today, in contrast, floor and roof trusses allow wide-open floor plans, and windows can be ordered in a staggering array of shapes and dimensions.

But if a new home is not carefully proportioned, these pieces may come together to resemble a suburban house rather than a charming old farmhouse.

Windows and white paint allow the sunroom to soar. This space is the
twin of the screen porch on the other side of the living room.

From the approach road, lanes and paths radiate to the various parts of the farm. A rail fence seems to corral the buildings as well as the animals.

The Ranch House Revisited

J ANE AND PETER'S HORSE FARM is at the end of the road—literally. The county road goes no farther than their place, located in Washington's northern Cascades, and the nearest neighbor is five miles away. Peter came across the remote site one weekend while hunting for a ranch where they could spend their retirement. The farm was abandoned, the original house having burned down years before, but the corrals and fenced pastures remained. The property was surrounded by a protected wilderness, which offered the possibility of horseback riding in the extensive forests and rolling grassland beyond the ranch's boundaries.

A Wide-Brimmed Roof

Jane and Peter also appreciated the existing barn with its 14-in.-wide siding and square-headed nails, as well as the assorted sheds. They wanted their new house to fit in with the community-like gathering of these unadorned outbuildings. Architect Stephen Rising was hired to come up with a complementary design, one

The farmhouse is a newcomer to this landscape; but with its relaxed attitude, the home fits right in with the existing outbuildings.

177

The open porch shades interior spaces from the hot summer sun, something like the broad brim of a cowboy hat. A well-designed porch not only offers shelter but also can frame an inviting entrance to the home.

that combined a simple footprint with a single, symmetrical roof form.

The home that resulted is clad in straight-forward materials often used in farm buildings—board-and-batten siding and a roof of corrugated metal. The shape of the hipped roof is somewhat unusual for a ranch house, however, with a lower pitch wrapping around all four sides. This skirt-like section covers a porch that provides shade in

the hot, dry summers and also buffers the home from the snows of the region's rugged winters. The roof even seems to echo the slopes of the surrounding mountains.

The road to the ranch ends in a circular drive that serves the barn, workshop, sheds, corrals, garage, and house. Visitors are welcomed by the home's long, wraparound front porch and the red front door. The green pasture rolls right up to the edge of the porch, which is set only two steps off the ground. It's easy to imagine one of the horses from the adjacent field tethered to a hand-hewn post while the rider takes a break in the shade. Much as the porch is an in-between space, the hand-peeled finish on its log posts falls appropriately between a raw, natural material and a smoothly milled column.

Dressing Down with Board and Batten

Board-and-batten siding is a traditional way of cladding buildings. It is made up of wide vertical boards with narrower strips, called battens, placed over their joints. This type of cladding is relatively easy to install, requiring no special tools or trade knowledge. It is a simple, economical way to side a shed or barn—or house. Because the boards and battens are applied from top to bottom, there are no ledges on which water can collect, meaning greater durability.

The orientation of the boards emphasizes the vertical proportions of buildings, so that they seem to be standing up proud on the open landscape. A contemporary way to achieve the look is to cover the walls with 4-ft. by 8-ft. plywood sheets and then place battens at regular intervals. The work goes quickly and the materials are less expensive than conventional lumber. This was the variation used on the home shown here. The siding gives the house a casual, informal appearance suggestive of a renovated barn.

With its assortment of chairs, benches, and rocker, the porch creates an almost seamless transition from house to pasture. Just as the porch is an in-between space, the peeled log posts are a transition between the trees on the property and the finished milled lumber inside.

The solid cedar front door is of the traditional cross-buck design you might expect to find on a ranch. Two sidelights illuminate the entry hall.

The timber frame, cabinets, and trim have a warmth that contrasts with the cool, flat drywall surfaces. The main living space is anchored by the granite fireplace, constructed to look as though stacked without mortar.

The centrally located stair works as an architectural feature, incorporating bookshelves below and a nook for the piano. The landing serves as a stage for the grandchildren's theatrical productions.

Site Considerations

FARMHOUSES OFTEN LOOK THE PART because of their association with nearby utility buildings. So siting a new house on an old farm is a critical first step in the design process. The spaces between the buildings can be thought of as outdoor rooms and the paths and roads as hallways.

As is typical of older homesteads in the northern Cascades, this farm is set in a protected hollow that seems to cradle the little settlement. The new house could have been perched up high along a mountain ridge to provide dramatic views, but the owners preferred to leave the horizon in its natural state.

SITE PLAN

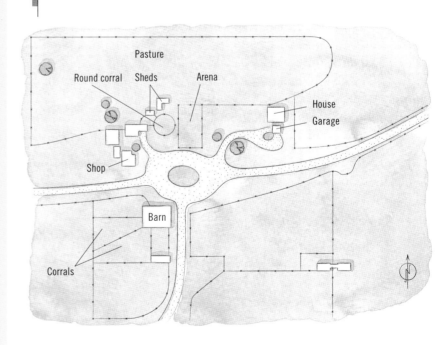

Natural Ingredients

Inside the house, Douglas fir posts and beams are exposed like those in an old barn. These structural elements delineate a central space encompassing the entry, stair, living room, and kitchen. The living room fireplace is made of local granite, with a monolithic stone hearth that looks like an outcrop from the surrounding hills. The stonework extends beyond the fireplace to support a window seat at one end and to surround the television cabinet on the other. The cool gray stone sets off the warm golden hues of the Douglas fir and cork floors.

The home's layout is designed for informal living. The kitchen is open to the living room; however, bookshelves on one side of the kitchen island help hide food prep clutter. A side door and window connect the kitchen to a sunroom

The inviting window seat, set on top of a rustic stone base, forms an integral part of the fireplace wall. A built-in bookshelf is close at hand.

An interior window brings light, views, and fresh air from the sunroom to the kitchen. The window doubles as a pass-through when moving food and dishes out to the sunroom table.

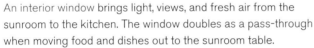

that can double as an intimate place to eat; its windows are replaced with screens in the warmer months, and a door links to the outside porch.

The dining room feels distinctly separate in its corner of the home. It assumes a more formal air because of the dark-hued walls and the tray-like coffered ceiling. The unusually long table can seat a large clan for either cowboy break-fasts in summertime or dressy Christmas dinners in winter.

Clearly, the focus of this home is the surrounding land. The office occupies a corner with wraparound windows that allow Jane and Peter to keep an eye on the entry drive and corrals. The master bedroom has its own door to the porch. Both it and the second-floor guest bedroom are at the back of the house, with quiet views toward the pasture on the sloping hillside.

This connection to the outdoors helps explain why the house is characterized by a sense of overall spaciousness, even though the rooms are

A continuous band of windows wraps around the corner of the home office, offering views of the barn and corrals. The roof's deep overhang keeps direct sun out of the eyes and off of work surfaces.

While the dining room has cork floors, as do most of the rooms in the house, its coffered ceiling is more formal than the exposed timbers and decking used elsewhere.

In this farmhouse, even the tub has a commanding view. A framed panel of frosted glass screens the toilet from the rest of the room.

The master bedroom is subtly divided into two zones, bed and sitting areas, by a change in the ceiling overhead. Tongue-and-groove boards follow the slope of the lower-pitched roof, and drywall is used for the higher ceiling.

relatively modest in size. Exterior doors on three sides of the house and generous banks of windows visually extend the perimeter of the home, so that porches, corrals, and fenced pastures feel like additional living spaces.

A House for All Seasons

This is a home with two lives. In the summer, Jane and Peter call it a "free dude ranch" because children, grandchildren, and friends come in continuous, welcome waves to join the year-round residents—horses, chickens, cats, and a dog. In the winter, snow and books are the primary company. Anticipating this way of living, Steven designed the house to stretch and contract with the seasons.

In the cold months, Jane and Peter close the door to the sunroom, use the large dining room only on major holidays, and live in the core of the kitchen, living room, office, and master bedroom, surrounded by the bookshelves tucked throughout. In the spring, summer, and fall, the house expands. The sunroom converts to a screen porch, the dining room is used casually for any meal, the open porches become additional living spaces, and the upstairs guest bedroom is often occupied. The grandchildren are housed in a cabin up the hill with "cowhand bunks" stacked from floor to ceiling.

As Jane and Peter had hoped, the new house and garage work well both in form and in function. The two buildings rest comfortably within the hollow because they were intentionally situated in an informal, natural way, suggesting that these additions to the landscape are part of the homestead's gradual evolution.

Even so, the home is not without its conspicuously new details: Jane says the shiny aluminum roof is not aging quite fast enough to suit her. But time will pass pleasantly enough in this rural retreat with its drama of the changing seasons. Knee-high spring wildflowers give way to the golden brown hues of summer and fall, and winter blankets the farm in snow. With all of those porches and doors and windows to the outside, the natural world is never more than a step away.

A local blacksmith crafted the hand-wrought hardware that contributes to the rustic feel of this farmhouse. The attention given to the door's hardware is appreciated by the home-owners daily when this door closes with a satisfying thud.

Painted beadboard walls, wide-plank cedar floors, and a tongue-and-groove ceiling give the sunroom a porchlike quality that sets it apart from the core of the house. When the continuous band of double-hung windows is replaced with screens in the summer, the space feels as much a part of the outside as of the house itself.

Farmhouse Gumbo

This farmhouse doesn't demand attention. Its unassuming aspect is reinforced by the snug galvanized roof and the use of antique white paint. Because the porch wraps around all four sides, the front and back are defined by the driveway and path approaching the house.

THERE ARE NO RULES when creating a new farmhouse. This home in rural Mississippi is a melting pot of influences. Its exterior forms, details, and materials conjure images of French colonial houses, along with elements of French West Indies architecture. Steve and Karen, the owners, affectionately call it their "Southern shack," and the interior brings back memories of having gone to summer camp as kids.

Architect Ken Tate laid out the drive by walking different potential routes to the house. The home sits at the high point of the site and appears to be a cabin that was gradually added on to for more living space. There is a casual sense of impermanence about the place, perched on its freestanding piers. The hipped roof looks something like a tent that might be blown away by the next good gust of wind. The rafter tails are cut back so that the eaves of the roof seem unsupported from a distance, in a makeshift way. The house even seems to be dozing, an effect caused by a line of dark shutters just below the porch roof. And at the entry, a row of

Instead of using a modern exterior sheathing such as plywood to brace the frame, the architect called for traditional diagonal boards. This method of construction makes the house seem to be of an older vintage, and it adds an informal layer of texture to the walls.

187

The home's design suggests that a simple one-room structure was added onto over time; the living room, bedroom, and carport look like small buildings that were eventually linked together. In contrast to the open porch, the solid board-and-batten walls of the bedroom wing signal that this is a private area.

The French doors at the end of the bedroom hall are aligned with a path to the pool house, helping link the home with its surroundings. Plantings have been arranged in a way that reinforces the architecture and also defines the yard's hallways and rooms.

IN DETAIL

Tin Roof, Rusted

WHEN METAL ROOFS WERE INTRODUCED in the 1800s, they proved to be low cost, lightweight, and easy to maintain—features that made them especially popular for rural buildings. Architect Ken Tate was attracted to the way in which the metal roofs on modest Southern farmhouses take on a rusty character with age, but the roof on this home is of a modern material that will maintain its appearance. A small crimped V adds a visual shadow line that complements the board-and-batten siding.

closed shutters suggests that the house is buttoned down and may not even be occupied.

A Shack with a Story

The home is centered around what appears to be the original "shack." This is the living and dining area, and it comes across as at once grand and primitive. The ceiling of the room is 16 ft. high, and the space is illuminated by rows of French doors with transom windows. Although the dimensions are impressive, the exposed studs and diagonal sheathing of the walls do look like something remembered from a childhood summer. By leaving these structural elements open to view, Ken reinforced the relaxed character that the owners were after. The diagonal pattern is distinctive but not overwhelming, because the surfaces are all painted monochromatic white. The walls are not quite as casually constructed as they appear; there is a layer of insulation between interior and exterior surfaces. The simple fireplace is in keeping with the room—just an opening in a wide stucco mass.

The porch railing was kept simple to avoid detracting from the view. The height of the porch might have felt overwhelming, but this effect was counteracted by hanging a row of dark shutters and painting the ceiling gray.

In contrast with its high ceilings and carefully designed array of French doors and transom windows, the living room has shedlike walls of exposed studs. Consistent with the rest of the room, the fireplace is impressive in size but embellished by only the arched opening.

A section of the wraparound porch is enclosed with screens. The screen frames are of bleached wood, giving the impression that they are later additions to the painted porch—another suggestion that the original structure was altered over the years.

This unheated back entry is open to the elements, offering an in-between space with doors to the kitchen, laundry room, and foyer. The subtle checkerboard painted on the wood decking is a rougher version of the pattern found in the kitchen.

French doors on four sides of the room lead to the surrounding porch. The adjacent kitchen's modest size and isolated placement are clear departures from the large, centrally located kitchens typical of modern homes; this galley feels as though it were laid out in space claimed from the porch in a later renovation. Even the details of the kitchen support the story line that the house went through a remodeling sometime back in the 1960s; there are plastic-laminate cabinets with wire pulls, and the countertop has a retro chrome edge.

Continuing the home's evolution, the bedroom wing seems to have been tacked onto the core structure. The bedrooms are dramatic in their Spartan simplicity, again with exposed framing and a lot of white paint. Cottage-like furniture and pipe-frame beds are a good match with the frankness of the rooms' revealed structure. Tall ceilings help keep the rooms cool, as does the floor of finished concrete in the master

The bedrooms have the spare feel of bunk rooms at summer camp. However, the use of white for everything from walls to iron beds to bedspreads gives a smart, civilized air to the barebones structure.

In keeping with the rest of the house, the bathroom combines refined pedestal sinks and framed hung mirrors with the rawness of exposed bulb light fixtures.

FLOOR PLAN

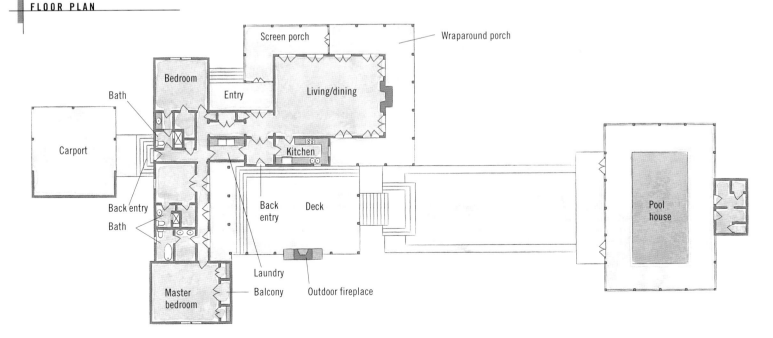

Screen porch

Wraparound porch

Bedroom

Entry

Living/dining

Bath

Carport

Kitchen

Back entry

Back entry

Deck

Pool house

Bath

Laundry

Master bedroom

Balcony

Outdoor fireplace

This bright passageway to the master bedroom is lined with French doors for an easy connection to the large deck. Throughout the house, interior walls are clad with the horizontal pickled boards visible at the far end of the hall.

bedroom. This bedroom also has its own balcony from which to check on the weather or shake a rug.

Degrees of Outside

The hall that serves the bedrooms has three sets of French doors opening onto a large deck that could be called an exterior living room because it is so integral with the house. Wings of the home define two sides of the deck, and a third is established by a large, sculptural masonry fireplace. The deck is elevated just high enough to provide a good view of an old cow pond behind the house, without being awkwardly perched above the ground.

Steve says that each space in the home is like "a different degree of outside" because the tall,

A French Influence

Early immigrants to America brought with them the building styles and construction methods of the country they left behind. While English-influenced farmhouses were common along the Eastern Seaboard, French colonists built distinctive homes in rural Louisiana and Mississippi. These houses, unlike those in the Northeast, were focused outdoors because of the moderate climate. Their thatched roofs were steeply pitched to help shed rainwater. Less typically, some houses had hipped roofs that kicked out at a lower angle. This lower section covered a wraparound porch, which was connected to the home's rooms by tall pairs of doors and windows. Houses often were set up on brick piers, both to allow breezes to circulate below and to keep bugs and the soil's humidity at a distance.

The home's entrances are gradual transitions between indoors and out. Here, a trellis covers the three sets of French doors opening to the principal deck and the master bedroom has its own small recessed balcony.

The masonry fireplace was finished with a thin coat of stucco to allow the courses of brick to show through, giving the impression of age.

airy rooms have fresh white walls that alternate with the paired French doors and transoms found in French colonial houses. The exposed framing gives the sense that the walls are thin and permeable, with little in the way of barrier between outdoors and in. In the French colonial fashion, the house is elevated to allow cooling breezes to pass below.

At the same time, the home feels secure and welcoming. Its variety of living spaces, inside and out, offers the family a niche for any mood, any time of day, any type of weather. A fictional narrative may have been used to guide the design, but the owners are now informing the home with their own real-life stories.

The large deck is bordered on two sides by the house's wings. With good lighting and a commanding fireplace to gather around, it serves as an outdoor living room.

Split-face concrete
block, used for walls
in the center of the
home and for the tall
chimney, has a practical,
no-nonsense character
in keeping with the cor-
rugated metal roof.

Barn Red and Edgy

ALTHOUGH THE COLOR of this Wyoming farmhouse is classic, undiluted barn red, the materials—concrete block, insulated wall panels, and manufactured wood beams—are
something else again. The endearingly eclectic design is the cre-
ation of the owners, Paul and Peggy Duncker, who served as both
architects and builders.

Both the interior and the exterior make conspicuous use of
split-faced concrete block. Ordinarily, concrete block is relegated
to the foundation, and whatever shows above grade is hidden behind foundation plantings; here, the material is used for entire
walls and even the fireplace. Another curiosity is that lofts on the
top floor can be reached only by a rolling ladder.

Most unusual of all might be the porch roof, which seems to sag
earthward and has been the source of many jokes about Paul's car-
pentry skills. Peggy claims that the slouch was the result of Paul
working overtime on the place, but in fact the couple had been influenced by the charmingly rickety state of farm structures in the
region. They decided to build in a suggestion of age from the start.

From a distance, the farmhouse shape is familiar and
the red clapboard looks entirely traditional. But on closer
inspection, this home's materials and detailing are unconventional and even whimsical.

Do-It-Yourself Ingenuity

WITH THE HANDS-ON APPROACH of old-time farmers, Paul and Peggy designed and also built their own house. Wearing these hats meant that they could experiment and improvise as they went along. The roof is corrugated steel, left with only its primer coat because the couple liked the worn-looking, muted finish and thought the material would hold up well in the dry alpine desert climate. The concrete block used inside and out has a low-tech agricultural sensibility, helping anchor the house to the site. The quirky angled porch and playfully composed windows add whimsy to the straightforward form.

Inside the house, economical materials take on an unexpected elegance. The concrete floor was poured in a 4-ft. grid and finished with boiled linseed oil. Tubes within the floor supply radiant heat without the clutter of conventional radiators. The kitchen island incorporates a countertop of clear-coated plate steel cut in a subtle curve. The main living space is framed with posts and beams laminated from wood chips; these are an environmentally friendly alternative to cutting down trees for lumber.

The half-bath takes advantage of another unusual material. The room is efficiently tucked under the stair but lacks a window, so the stair risers were made of sandblasted wire glass to share light from above without running the risk of breakage.

This can-do approach produces the eclectic variations and personal touches that distinguish farmhouses across the country. Paul and Peggy's house has the kind of endearing individuality that doesn't go out of style.

But the porch isn't pure whimsy—it helps shield the house from the elements and is a handy place to stack firewood as winter approaches.

To preserve the simple, unadorned shape of the home, the owners chose to have a detached garage. Viewed together, these two modest-size structures have a rural look, like a small farmstead. A larger home incorporating an attached garage might have resembled the conventional suburban designs Paul and Peggy wanted to avoid. Another advantage of a separate garage is that it could be placed on a side street along the couple's corner lot, leaving the front view of the house visually unencumbered.

Concrete at the Core

The design is a mix of tradition and innovation. While the home is reminiscent of a traditional farmhouse, with a steep gable roof, horizontal clapboard, and generous porch, the facades are playfully composed. Windows occur unpredictably in several shapes and sizes.

The house is boldly divided by a concrete block midsection, which protrudes on one side as the mudroom and on the other side as the base of a two-story stair tower. Because the block is insulated, it functions as the complete wall without the need for interior framing to contain insulation; the block's dark gray texture carries through to the inside, where it provides a contrasting texture to the smooth drywall.

A pegboard near the exterior mudroom door is another of this house's whimsical details. The yard implements and tools create an artful composition while being right at hand when needed.

While you'd expect to see shovels and barn boots by the back door of a working farm, in this home the equipment and clothing are recreational—but no less rugged. To meet the needs of an active family, the mudroom looks more like a high school locker room.

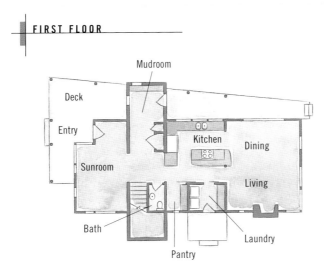

Mudroom

Deck

Entry

Kitchen

Dining

Sunroom

Living

Bath

Laundry

Pantry

The home's circulation and utility areas fall in this midsection, with the living spaces placed at the ends of the house so that they can take advantage of mountain views and daylight. The concrete core also effectively divides these ends into two zones, allowing Paul and Peggy to isolate the TV in the sunroom from conversations by the living room fireplace.

The rough concrete block wall of the mudroom reaches into the relative refinement of the sunroom, for an interesting meeting of formal and informal textures.

The white walls and ceiling are a neutral backdrop for the interesting materials and details incorporated in this home. Red birch cabinetry, sliding steel and glass barn doors, and exposed structural elements lend a creative, hands-on spirit to the house.

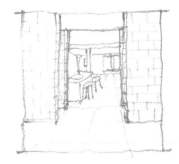

Open sight lines make a modest-size home feel larger. This loosely defined center aisle runs from front to back, making it easier to walk—and see—from one room to another.

Durable but not Drab

The ground floor is a concrete slab, poured over polyethylene tubing that circulates liquid to provide radiant heat. Under its coating of linseed oil, the slab will hold up well to traffic. It also warms the home comfortably, without the clutter of baseboard heating fixtures or the drying drafts characteristic of forced-air systems. Paul and Peggy made a clean break with farmhouses of the past in choosing a geothermal heat pump to provide the warmth for the system.

The activity of the home centers around the kitchen. The countertop is washed with light from a low strip of awning windows set just above the backsplash. This innovative arrangement leaves plenty of wall space above the windows for storing large bowls and pitchers and hanging utensils from hooks. The large island includes an elevated counter for light meals so that kitchen loungers are not in the way of food prep; the no-nonsense countertop is made of clear-coated plate steel, a high-tech surface that makes a visual link with the face of the stainless-steel refrigerator. Because the refrigerator doors are not magnetic, the couple clad the rolling pantry door in steel so that it can serve as a gallery wall for the young artists in the house. Next to the pantry, the sunny laundry room has a door made of plate steel and wire glass that obscures the clutter while sharing light with the kitchen.

A massive overhead beam spans the house at one end of the kitchen, marking where that

You don't need walls to define rooms. Furniture, lighting, and window composition can establish the boundary between one room and the next, as in this invisible dividing line between living and dining areas.

flat-ceilinged room gives way to the dining and living area. This space is under a shed roof, its ceiling beams open to view. Concrete block reappears in the fireplace, standing unrepentantly plain with a minimalist mantel ledge made of plate steel. The block continues on up through the roof to form a freestanding chimney so tall that it looks industrial from the outside. To bring in fresh air, operable clerestory windows are set above large fixed panes with views of the Grand Tetons. The nearby dining table sits silhouetted in front of a wall of glass that catches the western sun around the dinner hour.

A master suite, two bedrooms, and a bath occupy the second floor without wasting an inch—including the area that would have been eaten up by a stairway to the finished space under the

In the practical manner of a workshop, the tools of the kitchen are hung right out in plain sight. The wire glass in the cabinet doors and the stripped down, bare-bulb light fixtures express the commonsense design aesthetic of the owners.

The cedar siding has been stained, rather than painted, giving the house a more rustic look. Horizontal clapboard, vertical board-and-batten, and block all combine to enliven the facades of the home.

steeply pitched roof. In a novel solution, a ladder can be rolled on a track to access any of three areas on this level: a play loft above the kids' rooms, a storage room, or an office loft above the master suite. The lofts add a surprising degree of breathing space, making this compact house feel considerably larger.

Paul and Peggy's design is an unusual hybrid of practicality and whimsy, and it stands as an example of how an affordable home can also be generous, tactile, and funky. The house bridges the past and present as well. While its overtly modern sensibility catches your eye from the street, the home also fits right in with the adjacent hay fields and the legacy suggested by rusting farm implements in the yard.

Showing Your Tails

Roofs are supported by boards called rafters. In most houses today they are concealed above the ceiling and their lower ends (or tails) aren't visible from outside of the house. But in early homes, rafters might be left exposed on the inside, and their tails often continued to the edge of the roof's overhang.

Characteristically, the roof of this house combines old-tech with high-tech. Although the roof is framed with structural insulated panels—a sandwich of rigid insulation between two sheets of plywood—Paul and Peggy chose to add exposed rafter tails to emphasize the rural character of their unadorned home.

A sliding ladder is a novel space-saving device—not to mention a feature irresistible to kids.
The wall-mounted rail guides the ladder to three spaces just under the roof.

Shades of Shaker

The house seems comfortable with itself, the larger form appearing to lean casually on the smaller. While the composition of the smaller elements is carefully balanced, the whole is animated by its asymmetry.

THE PRIM WHITE FARMHOUSE isn't the only design legacy of agricultural America. When Judi and Gary set about building a farmhouse in the Berkshire Hills of western Massachusetts, they were drawn to the distinctive form of the barn.

As interpreted by architects Ann McCallum and Andy Burr, this home incorporates several barnlike features. Both the house and barn have inset porches that correspond to the sheltering bays found on the ground level of many barns. A typical farmhouse, on the other hand, might have a projecting porch with a shed or hipped roof. Another borrowed feature is the row of small, square windows placed just below the eaves of the standing-seam metal roof, which looks appropriate to a barn. Elsewhere, several ganged windows look as though they might be filling in the opening left by a tractor-sized door.

The barn has a garage on its lower level and two guest bedrooms above. Large sliding doors correspond to what would be a hayloft door, and custom-made ventilators crown the peak as on a traditional barn.

Wainscoting is in keeping with the practical, economical spirit of rural farmers. It preserves the lower walls from bumps and scrapes and visually ties together the rooms of the home.

Whatever the design lineage of Judi and Gary's house, it clearly can be identified as a residence as visitors approach. The large number of windows gives that away at once. Step inside, and the rooms have the traditional appointments of an older home, although carried out with a modern spirit. While the double-hung windows may be standard items, they are generous and ganged together to bring in lots of light and views of the property. On the second floor of the barn, the windows make up a wall of glass, filling in what would have been an opening for a hayloft door.

A Domesticated Barn

The lack of ornament also has the directness of an outbuilding. The main doors to the home are white, and as they're set within white walls they don't advertise themselves as being entries. The house is even free of the usual foundation plantings. Inside, the kitchen and living and dining areas are as open as a barn. The curved timber trusses were inspired by those used to support the roofs of medieval barns, although the tie rods spanning the space do the real work in this house.

The house and barn were positioned to create two sides of a courtyard, with a low stone wall completing the border. While most houses are oriented toward the driveway, Ann and Andy took a different tack: To preserve the intimacy of this outdoor room, they planned to have cars parked in or near the barn, making it necessary to walk across the courtyard to enter the house. Also, the enclosed yard works as a transition space between the shelter of the porch and the fields beyond.

IN DETAIL

Classic Clapboard

HORIZONTAL CLAPBOARD SIDING is a classic choice for cladding a farmhouse. Widths vary, but traditional siding typically has an exposure (or visible dimension) of about 4 in. The resulting texture gives walls a human scale, rather than creating a large, featureless plane. The overlapping boards naturally shed water. They usually run to vertical corner boards, avoiding the need to make mitered (angled) cuts at the ends of each board.

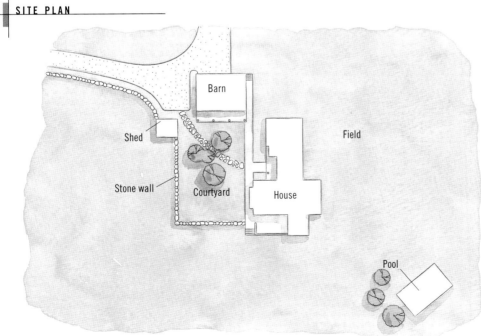

SITE PLAN

Shed

Barn

Field

Stone wall

Courtyard

House

Pool

Local hand-chiseled granite was used for the farmhouse's column and step. An old cowbell allows guests to announce themselves and is also used to call folks in to dinner.

The open spaces of the home call to mind a renovated barn, and the wood trusses lead the eye up to the vaulted tongue-and-groove ceiling. A row of large double-hung windows does the job of a picture window without veering too far from tradition.

Calm but not Static

The porch and the overhang of the barn are supported by columns of granite, a nod to the stone columns used in a nearby historic Shaker village. Inside, the simple woodwork includes wainscoting; its beadboard paneling and the drywall above are painted in soft, restful colors that set off the cap rail. The muted blues and greens used throughout the house are typical of the Shaker palette. The center hall stairway is not out of the ordinary, but again it is characterized by the quiet honesty of a piece of Shaker furniture.

The smaller of the home's two gabled forms holds the dramatic open space devoted to the main living area. The lower roof line in this part of the house keeps the space inside from being uncomfortably tall. The wood trusses overhead add warmth and animate the volume with their reassuring rhythm. A set of four floor-to-ceiling double-hung windows allows light to pour into

Guided by the Vernacular

When designing a new home in the manner of a farmhouse, consider taking inspiration from the *vernacular* architecture—buildings that evolved out of the practical needs and idiosyncrasies of a particular area. Look for forms, details, and materials that may be special to your region. These variations may hold up better in your climate. Also, by drawing on the local architectural language you can help a new house settle unobtrusively into the landscape.

The architecture in a nearby Shaker community influenced the design and colors of this new farmhouse, which is used as a second home. The focus on elegant, spare essentials seemed appropriate for a house that is regarded as an antidote to a hectic workweek in the city.

the living room. These south-facing windows have been shielded from the summer sun in a couple of effective ways: They are recessed slightly, and a small shed roof runs just above them. Insetting the windows also creates the impression that the exterior walls are of thick masonry, lending a feeling of gravity to the home. To either side, built-ins make practical use of the depth. The gable window high above is set within the wall to further suggest that the walls are unusually thick.

Along one side of the living room, a 4-ft.-high built-in cabinet conceals the television, holds a wood box with an access door to the outside, and surrounds the fireplace. The honesty of an exposed round metal flue appealed to Judi and Gary. So, in place of a traditional massive masonry chimney, the thin flue extends up in front of a band of windows running the length of the cabinet, maximizing daylight and views.

FIRST FLOOR

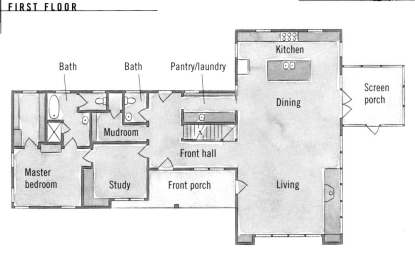

The efficient galley kitchen cuts down on the number of steps between each work station. A deep porcelain sink is in keeping with the style of the house. The unusually tall windows throw light onto the vaulted ceiling.

Daylight spills into the kitchen work area from windows on three sides. To avoid having the kitchen appear too conventional, the sage green upper cabinets and island have a furniture-like look that is intentionally different from the white base cabinets.

A Gathering Place for Family

The couple envisioned their new home as a magnet for visiting family, and the vaulted area is a particularly inviting place to gather. Even the kitchen incorporates oversized double-hung windows that rest on the backsplash, making it bright and cheerful. The kitchen island is topped with soapstone, a durable material that New England long has been known for. A low ledge on the island does a subtle job of hiding the clutter of dishes at the sink. Both the island and two wall-hung cabinets are a muted green, distinct from the white base cabinets. This helps the

The screen porch can be opened up as an annex to the dining area, but dark paint and a natural wood ceiling give it a distinctly different character from the interior of the house.

The bedrooms were designed to be just big enough for a bed and dresser, following the traditional notion that they are simply places in which to sleep rather than suites for lounging away the day.

The walk-through pantry makes up for the cabinet space sacrificed to allow for all of the kitchen windows. Adjustable open shelves store everything from canned goods to serving trays.

built-ins look as though they were individual pieces, added to the kitchen over time. The kitchen manages to avoid being cluttered because much of the storage is handled by a large walk-through pantry with its own sink.

The master bedroom suite is also on the first floor, so that the owners can enjoy the ease and convenience of one-level living. The farm then expands when people come to spend the night. The house is like an accordion, as Judi puts it. Visitors can go upstairs to a pair of guest bedrooms, each with its own bath; the bedrooms

From a distance, the white rail fence looks as though it might contain a corral for horses rather than a pool. Grass comes right up next to the simple stone coping that surrounds the pool, maintaining a rural feel for what is usually thought of as a fixture of suburban living.

share a sitting area that is used as a getaway space for time away from large gatherings. There are also two bedrooms on the second floor of the barn. This nearby structure functions as a wing of the house, sharing the same siding, roof material, and granite columns.

Gary says that because good architecture sets the keynote of the home, there has been less need to rely on interior accouterments for the home's character. In the Shaker tradition, the furnishings and color choices are kept simple. This means that the house is free to resonate with the surrounding landscape—with both the hilly countryside and the spirit of the now-vanished Shaker way of life.

Independent but adjacent structures on a property provide the opportunity to make outdoor rooms and to create away spaces that are just right for home offices, studios, or guest quarters.

Three structures, the house, the barn, and a small shed, give the impression of being a cluster of white farm buildings that have been built up over time.

Architects and Designers

DAVID BERS ARCHITECTURE
39 West 14th Street
New York, NY 10011
(212) 242-8401
www.davidbers.com
An Unsentimental Farmhouse (pp. 20–29)

CLARISSA ALLEN & MITCHELL POSIN
Allen Farm
421 South Road
Chilmark, MA 02535
(508) 645-9064
A Bicentennial Renovation (pp. 30–39)
Designer/builder: Mark Hurwitz
Company, Chilmark, MA

WARNER & ASMUS ARCHITECTS
St Paul, MN
(651) 647-6650
www.warnerasmus.com
Little Red Barn House (pp. 40–49)
Project team: Geoffrey Warner,
Jancis Curiskis, Joseph Lambert.
Builder: Bob Swan, Swanbuilt Homes,
Spooner, WI

RILL + DECKER ARCHITECTS, PC
5019 Wilson Lane, Suite 200
Bethesda, MD 20814
(301) 652-2484
www.rilldecker.com
Instant Evolution (pp. 50–59)
Principal architect: Anne Y. Decker, AIA
Builder: Hopkins & Porter, Potomac, MD
Interior designer: Debra Kernan,
Distinctive Designs, Potomac, MD
Landscape architect: Brian Kane,
The Kane Group, Alexandria, VA

DAVID S. GAST & ASSOCIATES
1746 Union Street
San Francisco, CA 94123
(415) 885-2946
www.dsga.com
Old Farmhouse, New Farmhouse (pp. 60–69)
Principal architect: David S. Gast, AIA
Interior designer:
Deborah Michie Interior Design, Fairfax, CA
Landscape architect:
Jack Chandler & Associates, Yountville, CA

NORVAL WHITE + ASSOCIATES
Au Chicot
32330 Mouchan, France
In the Image of a Barn (pp. 70–79)
Interior designer: Camilla White

WILLIAM MCDONALD ARCHITECT
P.O. Box 6671
San Antonio, TX 78209
(210) 281-9559
A Three-In-One Farmhouse (pp. 80–87)
Builder: Albert Tampke Construction,
Utopia, TX
Landscape architect: Terry Lewis Landscape
Architects, San Antonio, TX

HELIX/ARCHITECTURE + DESIGN
1629 Walnut
Kansas City, MO 64108
(816) 300-0300
www.wearehelix.com
Farmhouse with an Edge (pp. 88–97)
Project team: John Jesik, Kathy Kelly,
Bill Poole, Reeves Wiedeman
Interior designers: Helix/Architecture +
Design; Sheila G. Caramella, Woodstone
Interiors, Greensburg, PA

SALA ARCHITECTS
43 Main Street SE, Suite 410
Minneapolis, MN 55414
(612) 379-3037
www.salaarc.com
New Plot, Old Story (pp. 98–105)
Project team: Paul Buum, AIA,
Gregg Graton, AIA, and Dale Mulfinger, FAIA
Builder: Kyle Hunt and Partners,
Deep Haven, MN

ROBERT M. GURNEY, FAIA
113 South Patrick Street
Alexandria, VA 22314
(703) 739-3843
Blue Ridge Contrast (pp. 106–115)
Builder: Chris Stanton and Mike Puskar, MT
Puskar Construction Co., Alexandria, VA
Interior designer: Edward Perlman,
Washington, DC
Structural engineer: Tony Beale, Advanced
Engineers, Springfield, VA

DIXON WEINSTEIN ARCHITECTS
431 West Franklin Street
Chapel Hill, NC 27516
(919) 968-8333
www.dixonweinstein.com
A String of Barns (pp. 116–125)
General contractor: McLean Building Co.,
Chapel Hill, NC
Landscape architect: Sam Reynolds,
Reynolds & Jewell, Raleigh, NC

MEYER, SCHERER & ROCKCASTLE, LTD.
710 South Second Street, 7th Floor
Minneapolis, MN 55401
(612) 375-0336
www.msrltd.com
A Farmhouse Takes Wing (pp. 126–135)
Principal architect: Thomas Meyer, AIA
Builder: Greg W. Olson, Schafer, MN
Interior designer: Lynn Barnhouse, CID, Meyer,
Scherer & Rockcastle, Ltd.
Landscape architect: Herb Baldwin, Jordan, MN

EL DORADO ARCHITECTS
1907-C Wyandotte Trafficway
Kansas City, MO 64108
(816) 474-3838
eldoradoarchitects.com
Barn with a Past and Future (pp. 136–145)
Principal architect: Dan Magin
Landscape and interior design: Dan Magin;
Ann Willoughby, Willoughby Design Group,
Kansas City, MO

TCA ARCHITECTURE
6211 Roosevelt Way NE
Seattle, WA 98115
(206) 522-3830
www.tca-inc.com
The Ranch House Revisited (pp. 176–185)
Principal architect: Steve Rising

CARROLL ARCHITECTS
4 South Union Street, 2nd Floor
Lambertville, NJ 08530
(609) 397-0095
www.carrollarchitects.net
A Farm Full of Projects (pp. 146–155)
Builder: Wayne Castle, NJ

KEN TATE ARCHITECT
206 Covington Street
P.O. Box 550
Madisonville, LA 70447
(985) 845-8181
www.kentatearchitect.com
Farmhouse Gumbo (pp. 186–193)
Builders: R.E. Turner Construction, Pearl, MS;
Craig-Wilkinson Inc., Jackson, MS
Landscape architect: Philip Watson,
Fredericksburg, VA

PATRICIA MOTZKIN ARCHITECTURE
2927 Newbury Street
Berkeley, CA 94703
(510) 649-7709
Pavilions in the Pasture (pp. 156–165)
Builder: Tavis Construction, Santa Rosa, CA

TOBLER DUNCKER ARCHITECTS
P.O. Box 4735
Jackson, WY 83001
(307) 733-7303
Barn Red and Edgy (pp. 194–203)
Principal architect: Peggy Duncker
Design/builder: Paul Duncker, HandsOn
Design, Wilson, WY

TIGERMAN MCCURRY ARCHITECTS
444 North Wells Street, Suite 206
Chicago, IL 60610
(312) 644-5880
www.tigerman-mccurry.com
Farmhouse As Fun House (pp. 166–175)
Builder: Greg Kaiser, Dunes Development,
Lakeside, MI
Interior designers: Margaret McCurry and
Betty Lu Saltzman

BURR AND MCCALLUM ARCHITECTS
720 Main Street
P.O. Box 345
Williamstown, MA 01267
(413) 458-2121
www.burrandmccallum.com
Shades of Shaker (pp. 204–213)
Builder: Albert Cummings, Williamstown, MA

REHKAMP LARSON ARCHITECTS
2732 West 43rd Street
Minneapolis, MN 55410
(612) 285-7275
www.rehkamplarson.com
Introduction (pp. 2–3)

ALEXANDER DESIGN STUDIO
8212 Main Street
Ellicott City, MD 21043
(410) 465-8207
pp. 7, 12 (bottom), 14 (top), 16 (bottom)

SALA ARCHITECTS
904 South 4th Street
Stillwater, MN 55082
(651) 351-0961
www.salaarc.com
Principal architect: Wayne Branum, AIA
An American Icon
pp. 8, 10 (bottom left), 16 (top left, top right),
17 (bottom)